H. Clay

Engraved by W. H. Dougal, by permission for the use of Congress,
from a Bust by H. K. Brown of N.Y. in the possession of Cadwalader Ringgold U.S.N.
Daguerreotype by Whitehurst.

WASHINGTON, D.C.

1852

Printed by H.C. Beaner.

OBITUARY ADDRESSES

ON THE

OCCASION OF THE DEATH

OF THE

HON. HENRY CLAY,

A SENATOR OF THE UNITED STATES FROM THE STATE OF KENTUCKY,

DELIVERED IN THE

Senate and in the House of Representatives of the United States,

JUNE 30, 1852,

AND THE

FUNERAL SERMON OF THE REV. C. M. BUTLER,

CHAPLAIN OF THE SENATE,

PREACHED IN THE SENATE, JULY 1, 1852.

Printed by order of the Senate and House of Representatives.

WASHINGTON:
PRINTED BY ROBERT ARMSTRONG.
1852.

SENATE OF THE UNITED STATES.

July 2, 1852.

Mr. Mangum submitted the following resolution, which was considered, by unanimous consent, and agreed to:—

Resolved, That the Committee of Arrangements cause to be published in a pamphlet form, and in such manner as may seem to them appropriate, for the use of the Senate, ten thousand copies of the addresses made by the members of the Senate, and members of the House of Representatives, together with the discourse of the Rev. Dr. Butler, upon the occasion of the death of the Hon. Henry Clay.

Attest,

Asbury Dickins,

Secretary.

OBITUARY ADDRESSES.

SENATE OF THE UNITED STATES,

WEDNESDAY, JUNE 30, 1852.

After the reading of the Journal, Mr. UNDERWOOD rose, and addressed the Senate, as follows:

Mr. PRESIDENT: I rise to announce the death of my colleague, Mr. CLAY. He died at his lodgings, in the National Hotel of this city, at seventeen minutes past eleven o'clock yesterday morning, in the seventy-sixth year of his age. He expired with perfect composure, and without a groan or struggle.

By his death our country has lost one of its most eminent citizens and statesmen; and, I think, its greatest genius. I shall not detain the Senate by narrating the transactions of his long and useful life. His distinguished services as a statesman are inseparably connected with the history of his country. As Representative and Speaker in the other House of Congress, as Senator in this body, as Secretary of State, and as Envoy abroad, he has, in all these positions, exhibited a wisdom and patriotism which have made a deep and lasting impression upon the grateful hearts of his countrymen. His thoughts and his actions have already been published to the world in written biography; in Congressional debates and reports; in the Journals of the two Houses; and in the pages of American history. They have been commemorated by monuments erected on the wayside. They have been engraven on medals of gold. Their memory will survive the monuments of marble and the medals of gold; for these are effaced and decay by the friction of ages. But the thoughts and actions of my late colleague have become identified with the immortality of the human mind, and will pass down from generation to generation as a portion of our national inheritance, incapable of annihilation so long as genius has an admirer, or liberty a friend.

Mr. PRESIDENT, the character of HENRY CLAY was formed and developed by the influence of our free institutions. His physical, mental, and moral faculties were the gift of God. That they were greatly superior to the faculties allotted to most men cannot be questioned. They were not cultivated, improved, and directed by a liberal or collegiate education. His respectable parents were not wealthy, and had not the means of maintaining their children at college. Moreover, his father died when he was a boy. At an early period, Mr. CLAY was thrown upon his own resources, without patrimony. He grew up in a clerk's office in Richmond, Virginia. He there studied law. He emigrated from his native State and settled in Lexington, Kentucky, where he commenced the practice of his profession before he was of full age.

The road to wealth, to honour, and fame, was open before him. Under our Constitution and laws he might freely employ his great faculties unobstructed by legal impediments, and unaided by exclusive privileges. Very soon Mr. CLAY made a deep and favourable impression upon the people among whom he began his career. The excellence of his natural faculties was soon displayed. Necessity stimulated him in their cultivation. His assiduity, skill, and fidelity in professional engagements secured public confidence. He was elected member of the Legislature of Kentucky, in which body he served several sessions prior to 1806. In that year he was elevated to a seat in the Senate of the United States.

At the bar and in the General Assembly of Kentucky, Mr. CLAY first manifested those high qualities as a public speaker which have secured to him so much popular applause and admiration. His physical and mental organization eminently qualified him to become a great and impressive orator. His person was tall, slender, and commanding. His temperament ardent, fearless, and full of hope. His countenance clear, expressive, and variable—indicating the emotion which predominated at the moment with exact similitude. His voice, cultivated and modulated in harmony with the sentiment he desired to express, fell upon the ear like the melody of enrapturing music. His eye beaming with intelligence and flashing with coruscations of genius. His gestures and attitudes graceful and natural. These personal advantages won the prepossessions of an audience, even before his intellectual powers began to move his hearers; and when his strong common sense, his profound reasoning, his clear conceptions of his subject in all its bearings, and his striking and beautiful illustrations, united with such personal qualities, were brought to the discussion of any question, his audience was enraptured, convinced, and led by the orator as if enchanted by the lyre of Orpheus.

No man was ever blessed by his Creator with faculties of a higher order of excellence than those given to Mr. Clay. In the quickness of his perceptions, and the rapidity with which his conclusions were formed, he had few equals and no superior. He was eminently endowed with a nice discriminating taste for order, symmetry, and beauty. He detected in a moment every thing out of place or deficient in his room, upon his farm, in his own or the dress of others. He was a skilful judge of the form and qualities of his domestic animals, which he delighted to raise on his farm. I could give you instances of the quickness and minuteness of his keen faculty of observation which never overlooked any thing. A want of neatness and order was offensive to him. He was particular and neat in his handwriting, and his apparel. A slovenly blot or negligence of any sort met his condemnation; while he was so organized that he attended to, and arranged little things to please and gratify his natural love for neatness, order, and beauty, his great intellectual faculties grasped all the subjects of jurisprudence and politics with a facility amounting almost to intuition. As a lawyer, he stood at the head of his profession. As a statesman, his stand at the head of the Republican Whig party for nearly half a century, establishes his title to pre-eminence among his illustrious associates.

Mr. CLAY was deeply versed in all the springs of human action. He had read and studied biography and history. Shortly after I left college, I had occasion to call on him in Frankfort, where he was attending court, and well I remember to have found him with Plutarch's Lives in his hands. No one better than he knew how to avail himself of human motives, and all the circumstances which surrounded a subject, or could present them with more force and skill to accomplish the object of an argument.

Mr. CLAY, throughout his public career, was influenced by the loftiest patriotism. Confident in the truth of his convictions and the purity of his purposes, he was ardent, sometimes impetuous, in the pursuit of objects which he believed essential to the general welfare. Those who stood in his way were thrown aside without fear or ceremony. He never affected a courtier's deference to men or opinions which he thought hostile to the best interests of his country; and hence he may have wounded the vanity of those who thought themselves of consequence. It is certain, whatever the cause, that at one period of his life Mr. CLAY might have been referred to as proof that there is more truth than fiction in those profound lines of the poet—

"He who ascends the mountain top shall find
Its loftiest peaks most wrapt in clouds and snow;
He who surpasses or subdues mankind,
Must look down on the hate of those below:
Though far above the sun of glory glow,
And far beneath the earth and ocean spread.
Round him are icy rocks, and loudly blow
Contending tempests on his naked head,
And thus reward the toils which to those summits led."

Calumny and detraction emptied their vials upon him. But how glorious the change! He outlived malice and envy. He lived long enough to prove to the world that his ambition was no more than a holy aspiration to make his country the greatest, most powerful, and best governed on the earth. If he desired its highest office, it was because the greater power and influence resulting from such elevation would enable him to do more than he otherwise could for the progress and advancement—first of his own countrymen, then of his whole race. His sympathies embraced all. The African slave, the Creole of Spanish America, the children of renovated classic Greece—all families of men, without respect to color or clime, found in his expanded bosom and comprehensive intellect a friend of their elevation and amelioration. Such ambition as that, is God's implantation in the human heart for raising the down-trodden nations of the earth, and fitting them for regenerated existence in politics, in morals, and religion.

Bold and determined as Mr. CLAY was in all his actions, he was, nevertheless, conciliating. He did not obstinately adhere to things impracticable. If he could not accomplish the best, he contented himself with the nighest approach to it. He has been the great compromiser of those political agitations and opposing opinions which have, in the belief of thousands, at different times, endangered the perpetuity of our Federal Government and Union.

Mr. CLAY was no less remarkable for his admirable social qualities than for his intellectual abilities. As a companion, he was the delight of his friends; and no man ever had better or truer. They have loved him from the beginning, and loved him to the last. His hospitable mansion at Ashland was always open to their reception. No guest ever thence departed without feeling happier for his visit. But, alas! that hospitable mansion has already been converted into a house of mourning; already has intelligence of his death passed with electric velocity to that aged and now widowed lady who, for more than fifty years, bore to him all the endearing relations of wife, and whose feeble condition prevented her from joining him in this city, and soothing the anguish of life's last scene by those endearing attentions which no one can give so well as woman and a wife. May God infuse into her heart and mind the Christian spirit of submission under her bereavement! It cannot be long before she may expect a reunion in Heaven. A nation condoles with her and her children on account of their irreparable loss.

Mr. CLAY, from the nature of his disease, declined very gradually. He bore his protracted sufferings with great equanimity and patience. On one occasion, he said to me, that when death was inevitable and must soon come, and when the sufferer was ready to die, he did not perceive the wisdom of praying to be "delivered from sudden death." He thought under such circumstances the sooner suffering was relieved by death the better. He desired the termination of his own sufferings, while he acknowledged the duty of patiently waiting and abiding the pleasure of God. Mr. CLAY frequently spoke to me of his hope of eternal life, founded upon the merits of Jesus Christ as a Saviour; who, as he remarked, came into the world to bring "life and immortality to light." He was a member of the Episcopalian Church. In one of our conversations he told me, that as his hour of dissolution approached, he found that his affections were concentrating more and more upon his domestic circle—his wife and children. In my daily visits he was in the habit of asking me to detail to him the transactions of the Senate. This I did, and he manifested much interest in passing occurrences. His inquiries were less frequent as his end approached. For the week preceding his death he seemed to be altogether abstracted from the concerns of the world. When he became so low that he could not converse without being fatigued, he frequently requested those around him to converse. He would then quietly listen. He retained his mental faculties in great perfection. His memory remained perfect. He frequently mentioned events and conversations of recent occurrence, showing that he had a perfect recollection of what was said and done. He said to me that he was grateful to God for continuing to him the blessing of reason, which enabled him to contemplate and reflect on his situation. He manifested during his confinement the same characteristics which marked his conduct through the vigour of his life. He was exceedingly averse to give his friends "*trouble*," as he called it. Some time before he knew it, we commenced waiting through the night in an adjoining room. He said to me, after passing a painful day, "Perhaps some one had better remain all night in the parlour." From this time he knew some friend was constantly at hand ready to attend to him.

Mr. President, the majestic form of Mr. CLAY will no more grace these Halls. No more shall we hear that voice which has so often thrilled and charmed the assembled representatives of the American people. No more shall we see that waving hand and eye of light, as when he was engaged unfolding his policy in regard to the varied interests of our growing and mighty republican empire. His voice is silent on earth for ever. The darkness of death has obscured the lustre of his eye. But the memory of his services—not only to his beloved Kentucky, not only to the United States, but for the cause of human freedom and progress throughout the world—will live through future ages, as a bright example, stimulating and encouraging his own countrymen and the people of all nations in their patriotic devotions to country and humanity.

With Christians, there is yet a nobler and a higher thought in regard to Mr. CLAY. They will think of him in connection with eternity. They will contemplate his immortal spirit occupying its true relative magnitude among the moral stars of glory in the presence of God. They will think of him as having fulfilled the duties allotted to him on earth, having been regenerated by Divine grace, and having passed through the valley of the shadow of death, and reached an everlasting and happy home in that "house not made with hands, eternal in the heavens."

On Sunday morning last, I was watching alone at Mr. CLAY'S bedside. For the last hour he had been unusually quiet, and I thought he was sleeping. In that, however, he told me I was mistaken. Opening his eyes and looking at me, he said, "Mr. Underwood, there may be some question where my remains shall be buried. Some persons may designate Frankfort. I wish to repose at the cemetery in Lexington, where many of my friends and connections are buried." My reply was, "I will endeavour to have your wish executed."

I now ask the Senate to have his corpse transmitted to Lexington, Kentucky, for sepulture. Let him sleep with the dead of that city, in and near which his home has been for more than half a century. For the people of Lexington, the living and the dead, he manifested, by the statement made to me, a pure and holy sympathy, and a desire to cleave unto them, as strong as that which bound Ruth to Naomi. It was his anxious wish to return to them before he died, and to realize what the daughter of Moab so strongly felt and beautifully expressed: "Thy people shall be my people, and thy God my God. Where thou diest will I die, and there will I be buried."

It is fit that the tomb of HENRY CLAY should be in the city of Lexington. In our Revolution, liberty's first libation-blood was poured out in a town of that name in Massachusetts. On hearing it, the pioneers of Kentucky consecrated the name, and applied it to the place where Mr. CLAY desired to be buried. The associations connected with the name harmonize with his character; and the monument erected to his memory at the spot selected by him will be visited by the votaries of genius and liberty with that reverence which is inspired at the tomb of Washington. Upon that monument let his epitaph be engraved.

Mr. President, I have availed myself of Doctor Johnson's paraphrase of the epitaph on Thomas Hanmer, with a few alterations and additions, to express in borrowed verse my admiration for the life and character of Mr. CLAY, and with this heart-tribute to the memory of my illustrious colleague I conclude my remarks:

Born when Freedom her stripes and stars unfurl'd,
When Revolution shook the startled world—
Heroes and sages taught his brilliant mind
To know and love the rights of all mankind.
"In life's first bloom his public toils began,
At once commenced the Senator and man:
In business dext'rous, weighty in debate,
Near fifty years he labour'd for the State.
In every speech persuasive wisdom flow'd,
In every act refulgent virtue glow'd;
Suspended faction ceased from rage and strife,
To hear his eloquence and praise his life.
Resistless merit fixed the Members' choice,
Who hail'd him Speaker with united voice."
His talents ripening with advancing years—
His wisdom growing with his public cares—
A chosen envoy, war's dark horrors cease,
And tides of carnage turn to streams of peace.

Conflicting principles, internal strife,
Tariff and slavery, disunion rife,
All are *compromised* by his great hand,
And beams of joy illuminate the land.
Patriot, Christian, Husband, Father, Friend,
Thy work of life achieved a glorious end!

I offer the following resolutions:—

Resolved, That a committee of six be appointed by the President of the Senate, to take order for superintending the funeral of HENRY CLAY, late a member of this body, which will take place to-morrow at twelve o'clock, M., and that the Senate will attend the same.

Resolved, That the members of the Senate, from a sincere desire of showing every mark of respect to the memory of the deceased, will go into mourning for one month by the usual mode of wearing crape on the left arm.

Resolved, As a further mark of respect entertained by the Senate for the memory of HENRY CLAY, and his long and distinguished services to his country, that his remains, in pursuance of the known wishes of his family, be removed to the place of sepulture selected by himself at Lexington, in Kentucky, in charge of the Sergeant at Arms, and attended by a committee of six Senators, to be appointed by the President of the Senate, who shall have full power to carry this resolution into effect.

Mr. CASS.

MR. PRESIDENT: Again has an impressive warning come to teach us, that in the midst of life we are in death. The ordinary labours of this Hall are suspended, and its contentions hushed, before the power of Him, who says to the storm of human passion, as He said of old to the waves of Galilee, PEACE, BE STILL. The lessons of His providence, severe as they may be, often become merciful dispensations, like that which is now spreading sorrow through the land, and which is reminding us that we have higher duties to fulfil, and graver responsibilities to encounter, than those that meet us here, when we lay our hands upon His holy word, and invoke His holy name, promising to be faithful to that Constitution, which He gave us in His mercy, and will withdraw only in the hour of our blindness and disobedience, and of His own wrath.

Another great man has fallen in our land, ripe indeed in years and in honours, but never dearer to the American people than when called from the theatre of his services and renown to that final bar where the lofty and the lowly must all meet at last.

I do not rise, upon this mournful occasion, to indulge in the language of panegyric. My regard for the memory of the dead, and for the obligations of the living, would equally rebuke such a course. The severity of truth is, at once, our proper duty and our best consolation. Born during the revolutionary struggle, our deceased associate was one of the few remaining public men who connect the present generation with the actors in the trying scenes of that eventful period, and whose names and deeds will soon be known only in the history of their country. He was another illustration, and a noble one, too, of the glorious equality of our institutions, which freely offer all their rewards to all who justly seek them; for he was the architect of his own fortune, having made his way in life by self-exertion; and he was an early adventurer in the great forest of the West, then a world of primitive vegetation, but now the abode of intelligence and religion, of prosperity and civilization. But he possessed that intellectual superiority which overcomes surrounding obstacles, and which local seclusion cannot long withhold from general knowledge and appreciation.

It is almost half a century since he passed through Chillicothe, then the seat of government of Ohio, where I was a member of the Legislature, on his way to take his place in this very body, which is now listening to this reminiscence, and to a feeble tribute of regard from one who then saw him for the first time, but who can never forget the impression he produced by the charms of his conversation, the frankness of his manner, and the high qualities with which he was endowed. Since then he has belonged to his country, and has taken a part, and a prominent part, both in peace and war, in all the great questions affecting her interest and her honour; and though it has been my fortune often to differ from him, yet I believe he was as pure a patriot as ever participated in the councils of a nation, anxious for the public good, and seeking to promote it, during all the vicissitudes of a long and eventful life. That he exercised a powerful influence, within the sphere of his action, through the whole country, indeed, we all feel and know; and we know, too, the eminent endowments to which he owed this high distinction. Frank and fearless in the expression of his opinion, and in the performance of his duties, with rare powers of eloquence, which never failed to rivet the attention of his auditory, and which always commanded admiration, even when they did not carry conviction —prompt in decision, and firm in action, and with a vigorous intellect, trained in the contests of a stirring life, and strengthened by enlarged experience and observation, joined withal to an ardent love of country, and to great purity of purpose,—these were the elements of his power and success; and we dwell upon them with mournful gratification now, when we shall soon follow him to the cold and silent tomb, where we shall commit "earth to earth, ashes to ashes, dust to dust," but with the blessed conviction of the truth of that Divine revelation which teaches us that there is life and hope beyond the narrow house, where we shall leave him alone to the mercy of his God and ours.

He has passed beyond the reach of human praise or censure; but the judgment of his contemporaries has preceded and pronounced the judgment of history, and his name and fame will shed lustre upon his country, and will be proudly cherished in the hearts of his countrymen for long ages to come. Yes, they will be cherished and freshly remembered, when these marble columns, that surround us, so often the witnesses of his triumph—but in a few brief hours, when his mortal frame, despoiled of the immortal spirit, shall rest under this dome for the last time, to become the witnesses of his defeat in that final contest, where the mightiest fall before the great destroyer—when these marble columns shall themselves have fallen, like all the works of man, leaving their broken fragments to tell the story of former magnificence, amid the very ruins which announce decay and desolation.

I was often with him during his last illness, when the world and the things of the world were fast fading away before him. He knew that the silver cord was almost loosened, and that the golden bowl was breaking at the fountain; but he was resigned to the will of Providence, feeling that He who gave has the right to take away, in His own good time and manner. After his duty to his Creator, and his anxiety for his family, his first care was for his country, and his first wish for the preservation and perpetuation of the Constitution and the Union—dear to him in the hour of death, as they had ever been in the vigour of life. Of that Constitution and Union, whose defence in the last and greatest crisis of their peril, had called forth all his energies, and stimulated those memorable and powerful exertions, which he who witnessed can never forget, and which no doubt hastened the final catastrophe a nation now deplores, with a sincerity and unanimity, not less honourable to themselves, than to the memory of the object of their affections. And when we shall enter that narrow valley, through which he has passed before us, and which leads to the judgment-seat of God, may we be able to say, through faith in his Son, our Saviour, and in the beautiful language of the hymn of the dying Christian—dying, but ever living, and triumphant—

> "The world recedes, it disappears—
> Heaven opens on my eyes! my ears
> With sounds seraphic ring;
> Lend, lend your wings! I mount—I fly!
> Oh, Grave! where is thy victory?
> Oh, Death! where is thy sting?"

"Let me die the death of the righteous, and let my last hour be like his."

Mr. Hunter.

Mr. President: We have heard, with deep sensibility, what has just fallen from the Senators who have preceded me. We have heard, sir, the voice of Kentucky—and, upon this occasion, she had a right to speak—in mingled accents of pride and sorrow; for it has rarely fallen to the lot of any State to lament the loss of such a son. But Virginia, too, is entitled to her place in this procession; for she cannot be supposed to be unmindful of the tie which bound her to the dead. When the earth opens to receive the mortal part which she gave to man, it is then that affection is eager to bury in its bosom every recollection but those of love and kindness. And, sir, when the last sensible tie is about to be severed, it is then that we look with anxious interest to the deeds of the life, and to the emanations of the heart and the mind, for those more enduring monuments which are the creations of an immortal nature.

In this instance, we can be at no loss for these. This land, sir, is full of the monuments of his genius. His memory is as imperishable as American history itself, for he was one of those who made it. Sir, he belonged to that marked class who are the men of their century; for it was his rare good fortune not only to have been endowed with the capacity to do great things, but to have enjoyed the opportunities of achieving them. I know, sir, it has been said and deplored, that he wanted some of the advantages of an early education; but it, perhaps, has not been remembered that, in many respects, he enjoyed such opportunities for mental training as can rarely fall to the lot of man. He had not a chance to learn as much from books, but he had such opportunities of learning from men as few have ever enjoyed. Sir, it is to be remembered that he was reared at a time when there was a state of society, in the commonwealth which gave him birth, such as has never been seen there before nor since. It was his early privilege to see how justice was administered by a Pendleton and a Wythe, with the last of whom he was in the daily habit of familiar intercourse. He had constant opportunities to observe how forensic questions were managed by a Marshall and a Wickham. He was old enough, too, to have heard and to have appreciated the eloquence of a Patrick Henry, and of George Keith Taylor. In short, sir, he lived in a society in which the examples of a Jefferson, and a Madison, and a Monroe were living influences, and on which the setting sun of a Washington cast the mild effulgence of its departing rays.

He was trained, too, as has been well said by the Senator from Michigan, [Mr. CASS,] at a period when the recent revolutionary struggle had given a more elevated tone to patriotism, and imparted a higher cast to public feeling and to public character. Such lessons were worth, perhaps, more to him than the whole encyclopedia of scholastic learning. Not only were the circumstances of his early training favourable to the development of his genius, but the theatre upon which he was thrown, was eminently propitious for its exercise. The circumstances of the early settlement of Kentucky, the generous, daring, and reckless character of the people—all fitted it to be the theatre for the display of those commanding qualities of heart and mind, which he so eminently possessed. There can be little doubt but that those people and their chosen leader exercised a mutual influence upon each other; and no one can be surprised that with his brave spirit and commanding eloquence, and fascinating address, he should have led not only there but elsewhere.

I did not know him, Mr. President, as you did, in the freshness of his prime, or in the full maturity of his manhood. I did not hear him, sir, as you have heard him, when his voice roused the spirit of his countrymen for war—when he cheered the drooping, when he rallied the doubting through all the vicissitudes of a long and doubtful contest. I have never seen him, sir, when, from the height of the chair, he ruled the House of Representatives by the energy of his will, or when upon the level of the floor he exercised a control almost as absolute, by the mastery of his intellect. When I first knew him, his sun had a little passed its zenith. The effacing hand of time had just begun to touch the lineaments of his manhood. But yet, sir, I saw enough of him to be able to realize what he might have been in the prime of his strength, and in the full vigour of his maturity. I saw him, sir, as you did, when he led the "opposition" during the administration of Mr. Van Buren. I had daily opportunities of witnessing the exhibition of his powers during the extra session under Mr. Tyler's administration. And I saw, as we all saw, in a recent contest, the exhibition of power on his part, which was most marvellous in one of his years.

Mr. President, he may not have had as much of analytic skill as some others, in dissecting a subject. It may be, perhaps, that he did not seek to look quite so far ahead as some who have been most distinguished for political forecast. But it may be truly said of Mr. CLAY, that he was no exaggerator. He looked at events through neither end of the telescope, but surveyed them with the natural and the naked eye. He had the capacity of seeing things as the people saw them, and of feeling things as the people felt them. He had, sir, beyond any other man whom I have ever seen, the true mesmeric touch of the orator—the rare art of transferring his impulses to others. Thoughts, feelings, emotions, came from the ready mould of his genius, radiant and glowing, and communicated their own warmth to every heart which received them. His, too, was the power of wielding the higher and intenser forms of passion with a majesty and an ease, which none but the great masters of the human heart can ever employ. It was his rare good fortune to have been one of those who form, as it were, a sensible link, a living tradition which connects one age with another, and through which one generation speaks its thoughts and feelings, and appeals to another. And, unfortunate is it for a country, when it ceases to possess such men, for it is to them that we chiefly owe the capacity to maintain the unity of the great Epos of human history, and preserve the consistency of political action.

Sir, it may be said that the grave is still new-made which covers the mortal remains of one of those great men who have been taken from our midst, and the earth is soon to open to receive another. I know not whether it can be said to be a matter of lamentation, so far as the dead are concerned, that the thread of this life has been clipped when once it had been fully spun. They escape the infirmities of age, and they leave an imperishable name behind them. The loss, sir, is not theirs, but ours; and a loss the more to be lamented that we see none to fill the places thus made vacant on the stage of public affairs. But it may be well for us, who have much more cause to mourn and to lament such deaths, to pause amidst the business of life for the purpose of contemplating the spectacle before us, and of drawing the moral from the passing event. It is when death seizes for its victims those who are, by "a head and shoulders, taller than all the rest," that we feel most deeply the uncertainty of human affairs, and that "the glories of our mortal state are shadows, not substantial things." It is, sir, in such instances as the present that we can best study by the light of example the true objects of life, and the wisest ends of human pursuit.

Mr. Hale.

Mr. President: I hope I shall not be considered obtrusive, if on this occasion for a brief moment, I mingle my humble voice with those that, with an ability that I shall neither attempt nor hope to equal, have sought to do justice to the worth and memory of the deceased, and at the same time appropriately to minister to the sympathies and sorrows of a stricken people. Sir, it is the teaching of inspiration that "no man liveth and no man *dieth* unto himself."

There is a lesson taught no less in the death than in the life of every man—eminently so in the case of one who has filled a large space and occupied a distinguished position in the thoughts and regard of his fellow-men. Particularly instructive at this time is the event which we now deplore, although the circumstances attending his decease are such as are calculated to assuage rather than aggravate the grief which it must necessarily cause. His time had fully come. The three score and ten marking the ordinary period of human life had for some years been passed, and, full of years and of honours, he has gone to his rest. And now, when the nation is marshalling itself for the contest which is to decide "who shall be greatest," as if to chasten our ambition, to restrain and subdue the violence of passion, to moderate our desires and elevate our hopes, we have the spectacle of one who, by the force of his intellect and the energy of his own purpose, had achieved a reputation which the highest official honours of the Republic might have illustrated, but could not have enhanced, laid low in death—as if, at the very outset of this political contest, on which the nation is now entering, to teach the ambitious and aspiring the vanity of human pursuit and end of earthly honour. But, sir, I do not intend to dwell on that moral which is taught by the silent lips and closed eye of the illustrious dead, with a force such as no man ever spoke with; but I shall leave the event, with its silent and mute eloquence, to impress its own appropriate teachings on the heart.

In the long and eventful life of Mr. CLAY, in the various positions which he occupied, in the many posts of public duty which he filled, in the many exhibitions which his history affords of untiring energy, of unsurpassed eloquence, and of devoted patriotism, it would be strange indeed if different minds, as they dwell upon the subject, were all to select the same incidents of his life as pre-eminently calculated to challenge admiration and respect.

Sir, my admiration—aye, my affection for Mr. CLAY—was won and secured many years since, even in my school-boy days—when his voice of counsel, encouragement, and sympathy was heard in the other Hall of this Capitol, in behalf of the struggling colonies of the southern portion of this continent, who, in pursuit of their inalienable rights, in imitation of our own forefathers, had unfurled the banner of liberty, and, regardless of consequences, had gallantly rushed into that contest where "life is lost, or freedom won." And again, sir, when Greece, rich in the memories of the past, awoke from the slumber of ages of oppression and centuries of shame, and resolved

"To call her virtues back, and conquer time and fate"—

there, over the plains of that classic land, above the din of battle and the clash of arms, mingling with the shouts of the victors and the groans of the vanquished, were heard the thrilling and stirring notes of that same eloquence, excited by a sympathy which knew no bounds, wide as the world, pleading the cause of Grecian liberty before the American Congress, as if to pay back to Greece the debt which every patriot and orator felt was her due. Sir, in the long and honourable career of the deceased, there are many events and circumstances upon which his friends and posterity will dwell with satisfaction and pride, but none which will preserve his memory with more unfading lustre to future ages than the course he pursued in the Spanish-American and Greek revolutions.

MR. CLEMENS.

MR. PRESIDENT: I should not have thought it necessary to add any thing to what has already been said, but for a request preferred by some of the friends of the deceased. I should have been content to mourn him in silence, and left it to other tongues to pronounce his eulogy. What I have now to say shall be brief—very brief.

Mr. President, it is now less than three short years ago since I first entered this body. At that period it numbered among its members many of the most illustrious statesmen this Republic has ever produced, or the world has ever known. Of the living, it is not my purpose to speak; but in that brief period, death has been busy here; and, as if to mark the feebleness of human things, his arrows have been aimed at the highest, the mightiest of us all. First, died CALHOUN. And well, sir, do I remember the deep feeling evinced on that occasion by him whose death has been announced here to-day, when he said: "I was his senior in years—in nothing else. In the course of nature I ought to have preceded him. It has been decreed otherwise; but I know that I shall linger here only a short time, and shall soon follow him." It was genius mourning over his younger brother, and too surely predicting his own approaching end.

He, too, is now gone from among us, and left none like him behind. That voice, whose every tone was music, is hushed and still. That clear, bright eye is dim and lustreless, and that breast, where grew and flourished every quality which could adorn and dignify our nature, is cold as the clod that soon must cover it. A few hours have wrought a mighty change—a change for which a lingering illness had, indeed, in some degree, prepared us; but which, nevertheless, will still fall upon the nation with crushing force. Many a sorrowing heart is now asking, as I did yesterday, when I heard the first sound of the funeral bell—

"And is he gone?—the pure of the purest,
The hand that upheld our bright banner the surest,
Is he gone from our struggles away?
But yesterday lending a people new life,
Cold, mute, in the coffin to-day."

Mr. President, this is an occasion when eulogy must fail to perform its office. The long life which is now ended is a history of glorious deeds too mighty for the tongue of praise. It is in the hearts of his countrymen that his best epitaph must be written. It is in the admiration of a world that his renown must be recorded. In that deep love of country which distinguished every period of his life, he may not have been unrivalled. In loftiness of intellect, he was not without his peers. The skill with which he touched every chord of the human heart may have been equalled. The iron will, the unbending firmness, the fearless courage, which marked his character, may have been shared by others. But where shall we go to find all these qualities united, concentrated, blended into one brilliant whole, and shedding a lustre upon one single head, which does not dazzle the beholder only because it attracts his love and demands his worship?

I scarcely know, sir, how far it may be allowable, upon an occasion like this, to refer to party struggles which have left wounds not yet entirely healed. I will venture, however, to suggest, that it should be a source of consolation to his friends that he lived long enough to see the full accomplishment of the last great work of his life, and to witness the total disappearance of that sectional tempest which threatened to whelm the Republic in ruins. Both the great parties of the country have agreed to stand upon the platform which he erected, and both of them have solemnly pledged themselves to maintain unimpaired the work of his hands. I doubt not the knowledge of this cheered him in his dying moments, and helped to steal away the pangs of dissolution.

Mr. President, if I knew any thing more that I could say, I would gladly utter it. To me, he was something more than kind, and I am called upon to mingle a private with the public grief. I wish that I could do something to add to his fame. But he built for himself a monument of immortality, and left to his friends no task but that of soothing their own sorrow for his loss. We pay to him the tribute of our tears. More we have no power to bestow. Patriotism, honour, genius, courage, have all come to strew their garlands about his tomb; and well they may, for he was the peer of them all.

Mr. Cooper.

Mr. President: It is not always by words that the living pay to the dead the sincerest and most eloquent tribute. The tears of a nation, flowing spontaneously over the grave of a public benefactor, is a more eloquent testimonial of his worth and of the affection and veneration of his countrymen, than the most highly-wrought eulogium of the most gifted tongue. The heart is not necessarily the fountain of words, but it is always the source of tears, whether of joy, gratitude, or grief. But sincere, truthful, and eloquent, as they are, they leave no permanent record of the virtues and greatness of him on whose tomb they are shed. As the dews of heaven falling at night are absorbed by the earth, or dried up by the morning sun, so the tears of a people, shed for their benefactor, disappear without leaving a trace to tell to future generations of the services, sacrifices, and virtues of him to whose memory they were a grateful tribute. But as homage paid to virtue is an incentive to it, it is right that the memory of the good, the great, and noble of the earth should be preserved and honoured.

The ambition, Mr. President, of the truly great, is more the hope of living in the memory and estimation of future ages than of possessing power in their own. It is this hope that stimulates them to perseverance; that enables them to encounter disappointment, ingratitude, and neglect, and to press on through toils, privations, and perils to the end. It was not the hope of discovering a world, over which he should himself exercise dominion, that sustained Columbus in all his trials. It was not for this he braved danger, disappointment, poverty, and reproach. It was not for this he subdued his native pride, wandered from kingdom to kingdom, kneeling at the feet of princes, a suppliant for means to prosecute his sublime enterprise. It was not for this, after having at last secured the patronage of Isabella, that he put off in his crazy and ill-appointed fleet into unknown seas, to struggle with storms and tempests, and the rage of a mutinous crew. It was another and nobler kind of ambition that stimulated him to contend with terror, superstition, and despair, and to press forward on his perilous course, when the needle in his compass, losing its polarity, seemed to unite with the fury of the elements and the insubordination of his crew in turning him back from his perilous but glorious undertaking. It was the hope which was realized at last, when his ungrateful country was compelled to inscribe, as an epitaph on his tomb—

"COLUMBUS HAS GIVEN A NEW WORLD TO THE KINGDOMS OF CASTILE AND LEON,"

that enabled him, at first, to brave so many disappointments, and at last, to conquer the multitude of perils that beset his pathway on the deep. This, sir, is the ambition of the truly great—not to achieve present fame, but future immortality. This being the case, it is befitting here to-day, to add to the life of HENRY CLAY the record of his death, signalized as it is by a nation's gratitude and grief. It is right that posterity should learn from us, the contemporaries of the illustrious deceased, that his virtues and services were appreciated by his country, and acknowledged by the tears of his countrymen poured out upon his grave.

The career of HENRY CLAY was a wonderful one. And what an illustration of the excellence of our institutions would a retrospect of his life afford! Born in an humble station, without any of the adventitious aids of fortune by which the obstructions on the road to fame are smoothed, he rose not only to the most exalted eminence of position, but likewise to the highest place in the affections of his countrymen. Taking into view the disadvantages of his early position, disadvantages against which he had always to contend, his career is without a parallel in the history of great men. To have seen him a youth, without friends or fortune, and with but a scanty education, who would have ventured to predict for him a course so brilliant and beneficent, and a fame so well deserved and enduring? Like the pine, which sometimes springs up amidst the rocks on the mountain side, with scarce a crevice in which to fix its roots, or soil to nourish them, but which, nevertheless, overtops all the trees of the surrounding forest, HENRY CLAY, by his own inherent, self-sustaining energy and genius, rose to an altitude of fame almost unequalled in the age in which he lived. As an orator, legislator, and statesman, he had no superior. All his faculties were remarkable, and in remarkable combination. Possessed of a brilliant genius and fertile imagination, his judgment was sound, discriminating, and eminently practical. Of an ardent and impetuous temperament, he was nevertheless persevering and firm of purpose. Frank, bold, and intrepid, he was cautious in providing against the contingencies and obstacles which might possibly rise up in the road to success. Generous, liberal, and entertaining broad and expanded views of national policy, in his legislative course he never transcended the limits of a wise economy.

But, Mr. President, of all his faculties, that of making friends and attaching them to him was the most remarkable and extraordinary. In this respect, he seemed to possess a sort of fascination, by which all who came into his presence were attracted towards, and bound to him by ties which neither time nor circumstances had power to dissolve or weaken. In the admiration of his friends was the recognition of the divinity of intellect; in their attachment to him a confession of his generous personal qualities and social virtues.

Of the public services of Mr. Clay, the present occasion affords no room for a sketch more extended than that which his respected colleague [Mr. UNDERWOOD] has presented. It is, however, sufficient to say, that for more than forty years he has been a prominent actor in the drama of American affairs. During the late war with England, his voice was more potent than any other in awakening the spirit of the country, infusing confidence into the people, and rendering available the resources for carrying on the contest. In our domestic controversies, threatening the peace of the country and the integrity of the Union, he has always been first to note danger as well as to suggest the means of averting it. When the waters of the great political deep were upheaved by the tempest of discord, and the ark of the Union, freighted with the hopes and destinies of freedom, tossing about on the raging billows, and drifting every moment nearer to the vortex which threatened to swallow it up, it was his clarion voice, rising above the storm, that admonished the crew of impending peril, and counselled the way to safety.

But, Mr. President, devotedly as he loved his country, his aspirations were not limited to its welfare alone. Wherever freedom had a votary, that votary had a friend in HENRY CLAY; and in the struggle of the Spanish colonies for independence he uttered words of encouragement which have become the mottos on the banners of freedom in every land. But neither the services which he has rendered his own country, nor his wishes for the welfare of others, nor his genius, nor the affection of friends, could turn aside the destroyer. No price could purchase exemption from the common lot of humanity. HENRY CLAY, the wise, the great, the gifted, had to die;

and his history is summed up in the biography which the Russian poet has prepared for all, kings and serfs;

> * * * * "born, living, dying,
> Quitting the still shore for the troubled wave,
> Struggling with storm-clouds, over shipwrecks flying,
> And casting anchor in the silent grave."

But though time would not spare him, there is still this of consolation: he died peacefully and happy, ripe in renown, full of years and of honours, and rich in the affections of his country. He had, too, the unspeakable satisfaction of closing his eyes whilst the country he had loved so much and served so well was still in the enjoyment of peace, happiness, union, and prosperity—still advancing in all the elements of wealth, greatness, and power.

I know, Mr. President, how unequal I have been to the apparently self-imposed task of presenting, in an appropriate manner, the merits of the illustrious deceased. But if I had remained silent on an occasion like this, when the hearts of my constituents are swelling with grief, I would have been disowned by them. It is for this reason—that of giving utterance to their feelings as well as of my own—that I have trespassed on the time of the Senate. I would that I could have spoken fitter words; but, such as they are, they were uttered by the tongue in response to the promptings of the heart.

Mr. Seward.

Mr. President: Fifty years ago, Henry Clay of Virginia, already adopted by Kentucky, then as youthful as himself, entered the service of his country, a Representative in the unpretending Legislature of that rising State; and having thenceforward, with ardour and constancy, pursued the gradual paths of an aspiring change through Halls of Congress, Foreign Courts and Executive Councils, he has now, with the cheerfulness of a patriot, and the serenity of a Christian, fitly closed his long and arduous career, here in the Senate, in the full presence of the Republic, looking down upon the scene with anxiety and alarm, not merely a Senator like one of us who yet remain in the Senate House, but filling that character which, though it had no authority of law and was assigned without suffrage, Augustus Cæsar nevertheless declared was above the title of Emperor, *Primus inter Illustres*—the Prince of the Senate.

Generals are tried, Mr. President, by examining the campaigns they have lost or won, and statesmen by reviewing the transactions in which they have been engaged. Hamilton would have been unknown to us, had there been no constitution to be created; as Brutus would have died in obscurity, had there been no Cæsar to be slain.

Colonization, Revolution, and Organization—three great acts in the drama of our National Progress—

had already passed when the Western Patriot appeared on the public stage. He entered in that next division of the majestic scenes which was marked by an inevitable reaction of political forces, a wild strife of factions and ruinous embarrassments in our foreign relations. This transition stage is always more perilous than any other in the career of nations, and especially in the career of Republics. It proved fatal to the Commonwealth in England. Scarcely any of the Spanish-American States have yet emerged from it; and more than once it has been sadly signalized by the ruin of the Republican cause in France.

The continuous administration of Washington and John Adams had closed under a cloud which had thrown a broad, dark shadow over the future; the nation was deeply indebted at home and abroad, and its credit was prostrate. The Revolutionary factions had given place to two inveterate parties, divided by a gulf which had been worn by the conflict in which the Constitution was adopted, and made broader and deeper by a war of prejudices concerning the merits of the belligerents in the great European struggle that then convulsed the civilized world. Our extraordinary political system was little more than an ingenious theory, not yet practically established. The union of the States was as yet only one of compact; for the political, social, and commercial necessities to which it was so marvelously adapted, and which, clustering thickly upon it, now render it indissoluble, had not then been broadly disclosed, nor had the habits of acquiescence and the sentiments of loyalty, always slow of growth, fully ripened. The bark that had gone to sea, thus unfurnished and untried, seemed quite certain to founder by reason of its own inherent frailty, even if it should escape unharmed in the great conflict of nations which acknowledged no claims of justice and tolerated no pretensions of neutrality. Moreover, the territory possessed by the nation was inadequate to commercial exigencies and indispensable social expansion; and yet no provision had been made for enlargement, nor for extending the political system over distant regions, inhabited or otherwise, which must inevitably be acquired. Nor could any such acquisition be made, without disturbing the carefully-adjusted balance of powers among the members of the confederacy.

These difficulties, Mr. President, although they grew less with time and by slow degrees, continued throughout the whole life of the statesman whose obsequies we are celebrating. Be it known, then, and I am sure that history will confirm the instruction, that Conservatism was the interest of the nation, and the responsibility of its Rulers, during the period in which he flourished. He was ardent, bold, generous, and even ambitious; and yet with a profound conviction of the true exigencies of the country, like Alexander Hamilton, he disciplined himself and trained a restless nation, that knew only self-control, to the rigorous practice of that often humiliating conservatism which its welfare and security in that particular crisis so imperiously demanded.

It could not happen, sir, to any citizen to have acted alone, nor even to have acted always the most conspicuous part in a trying period so long protracted. HENRY CLAY, therefore, shared the responsibilities of Government with not only his proper contemporaries, but also survivors of the Revolution, as well as also many who will succeed himself. Delicacy forbids the naming of those who retain their places here, but we may without impropriety recall among his compeers a Senator of vast resources and inflexible resolve, who has recently withdrawn from this Chamber, but I trust not altogether from public life, (Mr. BENTON); and another, who, surpassing all his contemporaries within his country, and even throughout the world, in proper eloquence of the Forum, now in autumnal years for a second times dignifies and adorns the highest seat in the Executive Council, (Mr. WEBSTER.) Passing by these eminent and noble men, the shades of Calhoun, John Quincy Adams, Jackson, Monroe, and Jefferson, rise up before us—statesmen whose living and local fame has ripened already into historical and world-wide renown.

Among geniuses so lofty as these, HENRY CLAY

bore a part in regulating the constitutional freedom of political debate; establishing that long-contested and most important line which divides the sovereignty of the several States from that of the States confederated; asserting the right of Neutrality, and vindicating it by a war against Great Britain, when that just but extreme measure became necessary; adjusting the terms on which that perilous yet honourable contest was brought to a peaceful close; perfecting the Army and the Navy, and the national fortifications; settling the fiscal and financial policy of the Government in more than one crisis of apparently threatened revolution; asserting and calling into exercise the powers of the Government for making and improving internal communications between the States; arousing and encouraging the Spanish-American Colonies on this Continent to throw off the foreign yoke, and to organize Governments on principles congenial to our own, and thus creating external bulwarks for our own national defence: establishing equal and impartial peace and amity with all existing maritime Powers; and extending the constitutional organization of Government over all the vast regions secured in his lifetime by purchase or by conquest, whereby the pillars of the Republic have been removed from the banks of the St. Mary to the borders of the Rio Grande, and from the margin of the Mississippi to the Pacific coast. We may not yet discuss here the wisdom of the several measures which have thus passed in review before us, nor of the positions which the deceased statesman assumed in regard to them, but we may without offence dwell upon the comprehensive results of them all.

The Union exists in absolute integrity, and the Republican system is in complete and triumphant development. Without having relinquished any part of their individuality, the States have more than doubled already, and are increasing in numbers and political strength and expansion more rapidly than ever before. Without having absorbed any State, or having even encroached on any State, the Confederation has opened itself so as to embrace all the new members who have come, and now with capacity for further and indefinite enlargements has become fixed, enduring, and perpetual. Although it was doubted only half a century ago whether our political system could be maintained at all, and whether, if maintained, it could guarantee the peace and happiness of society, it stands now confessed by the world the form of Government not only most adapted to Empire, but also most congenial with the constitution of Human Nature.

When we consider that the nation has been conducted to this haven, not only through stormy seas, but altogether, also, without a course and without a star; and when we consider moreover, the sum of happiness that has already been enjoyed by the

American People, and still more the influence which the great achievement is exerting for the advancement and melioration of the condition of mankind, we see at once that it might have satisfied the highest ambition to have been, no matter how humbly, concerned in so great transaction.

Certainly, sir, no one will assert that HENRY CLAY in that transaction performed an obscure or even a common part. On the contrary, from the day on which he entered the public service until that on which he passed the gates of death, he was never a follower, but always a leader; and he marshalled either the party which sustained or that which resisted every great measure, equally in the Senate and among the people. He led where duty seemed to him to indicate, reckless whether he encountered one President or twenty Presidents, whether he was opposed by factions or even by the whole people. Hence it has happened, that although that people are not yet agreed among themselves on the wisdom of all, or perhaps of even any of his great measures, yet they are nevertheless unanimous in acknowledging that he was at once the greatest, the most faithful and the most reliable of their statesmen. Here the effort at discriminating praise of HENRY CLAY, in regard to his public policy, must stop in this place, even on this sad occasion which awakens the ardent liberality of his generous survivors.

But his personal qualities may be discussed without apprehension. What were the elements of the success of that extraordinary man? You, sir, knew him longer and better than I, and I would prefer to hear you speak of them. He was indeed eloquent—all the world knows that. He held the keys to the hearts of his countrymen, and he turned the wards within them with a skill attained by no other master.

But eloquence was nevertheless only an instrument, and one of many that he used. His conversation, his gesture, his very look, was persuasive, seductive, irresistible. And his appliance of all these was courteous, patient and indefatigable. Defeat only inspired him with new resolution. He divided opposition by his assiduity of address, while he rallied and strengthened his own bands of supporters by the confidence of success which, feeling himself, he easily inspired among his followers. His affections were high, and pure, and generous, and the chiefest among them was that which the great Italian poet designated as the charity of native land. And in him that charity was an enduring and overpowering enthusiasm, and it influenced all his sentiments and conduct, rendering him more impartial between conflicting interests and sections than any other statesman who has lived since the Revolution. Thus with very great versatility of talent and the most catholic equality of favour, he identified every question, whether of domestic administration or foreign policy, with his own great name, and so became a perpetual Tribune of the people. He needed only to pronounce in favour of a measure or against it, here, and immediately popular enthusiasm, excited as by a magic wand, was felt, overcoming all opposition in the Senate Chamber.

In this way he wrought a change in our political system, that I think was not foreseen by its founders. He converted this branch of the Legislature from a negative position, or one of equilibrium between the Executive and the House of Representatives, into the active ruling power of the Republic. Only time can disclose whether this great innovation shall be beneficent, or even permanent.

Certainly, sir, the great lights of the Senate have set. The obscuration is not less palpable to the country than to us, who are left to grope our uncertain way here, as in a labyrinth, oppressed with self-distrust. The times, too, present new embarrassments. We are rising to another and a more sublime stage of natural progress,—that of expanding wealth and rapid territorial aggrandizement. Our institutions throw a broad shadow across the St. Lawrence, and stretching beyond the valley of Mexico, reaches even to the plains of Central America; while the Sandwich Islands and the shores of China recognise its renovating influence. Wherever that influence is felt, a desire for protection under those institutions is awakened. Expansion seems to be regulated, not by any difficulties of resistance, but by the moderation which results from our own internal constitution. No one knows how rapidly that restraint may give way. Who can tell how far or how fast it ought to yield? Commerce has brought the ancient continents near to us, and created necessities for new positions—perhaps connections or colonies there—and with the trade and friendship of the elder nations their conflicts and collisions are brought to our doors and to our hearts. Our sympathy kindles, our indifference extinguishes the fire of freedom in foreign lands. Before we shall be fully conscious that a change is going on in Europe, we may find ourselves once more divided by that eternal line of separation that leaves on the one side those of our citizens who obey the impulses of sympathy, while on the other are found those who submit only to the counsels of prudence. Even prudence will soon be required to decide whether distant regions, East and West, shall come under our own protection, or be left to aggrandize a rapidly spreading and hostile domain of despotism.

Sir, who among us is equal to these mighty questions? I fear there is no one. Nevertheless, the example of HENRY CLAY remains for our instruction. His genius has passed to the realms of light, but his virtues still live here for our emulation. With them there will remain also the protection and favour of the Most High, if by the practice of justice and the maintenance of freedom we shall deserve it. Let, then, the bier pass on. With sorrow, but not without hope, we will follow the revered form that it bears to its final resting place; and then, when that grave opens at our feet to receive such an inestimable treasure, we will invoke the God of our fathers to send us new guides, like him that is now withdrawn, and give us wisdom to obey their instructions.

Mr. Jones, of Iowa.

Mr. President: Of the vast number who mourn the departure of the great man whose voice has so often been heard in this Hall, I have peculiar cause to regret that dispensation which has removed him from among us. He was the guardian and director of my collegiate days; four of his sons were my collegemates and my warm friends. My intercourse with the father was that of a youth and a friendly adviser. I shall never cease to feel grateful to him—to his now heart-stricken and bereaved widow and children, for their many kindnesses to me during four or five years of my life. I had the pleasure of renewing my acquaintance with him, first, as a delegate in Congress, while he was a member of this body from 1835 to 1839, and again in 1848, as a member of this branch of Congress; and during the whole of which period, some eight years, none but the most kindly feeling existed between us.

As an humble and unimportant Senator, it was my fortune to coöperate with him throughout the whole of the exciting session of 1849–'50—the labour and excitement of which is said to have precipitated his decease. That coöperation did not end with the accordant vote on this floor, but, in consequence of the unyielding opposition to the series of measures known as the "compromise," extended to many private meetings held by its friends, at all of which Mr. CLAY was present. And whether in public or private life, he everywhere continued to inspire me with the most exalted estimate of his patriotism and statesmanship. Never shall I forget the many ardent appeals he made to Senators, in and out of the Senate, in favour of the settlement of our then unhappy sectional differences.

Immediately after the close of that memorable session of Congress, during which the nation beheld his great and almost superhuman efforts upon this floor to sustain the wise counsels of the "Father of his Country," I accompanied him home to Ashland, at his invitation, to revisit the place where my happiest days had been spent, with the friends who there continued to reside. During that, to me, most agreeable and instructive journey, in many conversations he evinced the utmost solicitude for the welfare and honour of the Republic, all tending to show that he believed the happiness of the people and the cause of liberty throughout the world depended upon the continuance of our glorious Union, and the avoidance of those sectional dissensions which could but alienate the affections of one portion of the people from another. With the sincerity and fervour of a true patriot, he warned his companions in that journey to withhold all aid from men who laboured, and from every cause which tended, to sow the seeds of disunion in the land; and to oppose such, he declared himself willing to forego all the ties and associations of mere party.

At a subsequent period, sir, this friend of my youth, at my earnest and repeated entreaties, consented to take a sea voyage from New York to Havana. He remained at the latter place a fortnight, and then returned by New Orleans to Ashland. That excursion by sea, he assured me, contributed much to relieve him from the sufferings occasioned by the disease which has just terminated his eventful and glorious life. Would to Heaven that he could have been persuaded to abandon his duties as a Senator, and to have remained during the past winter and spring upon that Island of Cuba! The country would not now, perhaps, have been called to mourn his loss.

In some matters of policy connected with the administration of our general government, I have disagreed with him, yet the purity and sincerity of his motives I never doubted; and as a true lover of his country, as an honourable and honest man, I trust his example will be reverenced and followed by the men of this, and of succeeding generations.

Mr. Brooke.

Mr. President: As an ardent, personal admirer and political friend of the distinguished dead, I claim the privilege of adding my humble tribute of respect to his memory, and of joining in the general expression of sorrow that has gone forth from this Chamber. Death, at all times, is an instructive monitor as well as a mournful messenger; but when his fatal shaft hath stricken down the great in intellect and renown, how doubly impressive the lesson that it brings home to the heart that the grave is the common lot of all—the great leveller of all earthly distinctions! But at the same time we are taught that in one sense the good and great can never die; for the memory of their virtues and their bright example will live through all coming time in an immortality that blooms beyond the grave. The consolation of this thought may calm our sorrow; and, in the language of one of our own poets, it may be asked:

"Why weep ye, then, for him, who having run
The bound of man's appointed years, at last,
Life's blessings all enjoyed, life's labours done,
Serenely to his final rest has pass'd;
While the soft memory of his virtues yet
Lingers, like twilight hues when the bright sun has set?"

It will be doing no injustice, sir, to the living or the dead to say, that no better specimen of the true

American character can be found in our history than that of Mr. CLAY. With no adventitious advantages of birth or fortune, he won his way by the efforts of his own genius to the highest distinction and honour. Ardently attached to the principles of civil and religious liberty, patriotism was with him both a passion and a sentiment—a passion that gave energy to his ambition, and a sentiment that pervaded all his thoughts and actions, concentrating them upon his country as the idol of his heart. The bold and manly frankness in the expression of his opinions which always characterized him, has often been the subject of remark; and in all his victories it may be truly said he never "stooped to conquer." In his long and brilliant political career, personal considerations never for a single instant caused him to swerve from the strict line of duty, and none have ever doubted his deep sincerity in that memorable expression to Mr. Preston, "Sir, I had rather be right than be President."

This is not the time nor occasion, sir, to enter into a detail of the public services of Mr. CLAY, interwoven as they are with the history of the country for half a century; but I cannot refrain from adverting to the last crowning act of his glorious life—his great effort in the Thirty-first Congress for the preservation of the peace and integrity of this great Republic, as it was this effort that shattered his bodily strength, and hastened the consummation of death. The Union of the States, as being essential to our prosperity and happiness, was the paramount proposition in his political creed, and the slightest symptom of danger to its perpetuity filled him with alarm, and called forth all the energies of his body and mind. In his earlier life he had met this danger and overcome it. In the conflict of contending factions it again appeared; and coming forth from the repose of private life, to which age and infirmity had carried him, with unabated strength of intellect, he again entered upon the arena of political strife, and again success crowned his efforts, and peace and harmony were restored to a distracted people. But unequal to the mighty struggle, his bodily strength sank beneath it, and he retired from the field of his glory to yield up his life as a holy sacrifice to his beloved country. It has well been said that peace has its victories as well as war; and how bright upon the page of history will be the record of this great victory of intellect, of reason, and of moral suasion, over the spirit of discord and sectional animosities!

We this day, Mr. President, commit his memory to the regard and affection of his admiring countrymen. It is a consolation to them and to us to know that he died in full possession of his glorious intellect, and, what is better, in the enjoyment of that "peace which the world can neither give nor take away." He sank to rest as the full-orbed king of day, unshorn of a single beam, or rather like the planet of morning, his brightness was but eclipsed by the opening to him of a more full and perfect day—

> "No waning of fire, no paling of ray,
> But rising, still rising, as passing away.
> Farewell, gallant eagle, thou'rt buried in light—
> God speed thee to heaven, lost star of our night."

The Resolutions submitted by Mr. UNDERWOOD, were then unanimously agreed to.

Ordered, That the Secretary communicate these Resolutions to the House of Representatives.

On motion by Mr. UNDERWOOD,

Resolved, That, as an additional mark of respect to the memory of the deceased, the Senate do now adjourn.

HOUSE OF REPRESENTATIVES.

WEDNESDAY, JUNE 30, 1852.

The Journal of yesterday having been read,

A message was received from the Senate, by ASBURY DICKINS, Esq., its Secretary, communicating information of the death of HENRY CLAY, late Senator from the State of Kentucky, and the proceedings of the Senate thereon.

The resolutions of the Senate having been read,

Mr. BRECKINRIDGE then rose and said:

Mr. SPEAKER: I rise to perform the melancholy duty of announcing to this body the death of HENRY CLAY, late a Senator in Congress from the Commonwealth of Kentucky.

Mr. CLAY expired at his lodgings in this city yesterday morning, at seventeen minutes past eleven o'clock, in the seventy-sixth year of his age. His noble intellect was unclouded to the last. After protracted sufferings, he passed away without pain; and so gently did the spirit leave his frame, that the moment of departure was not observed by the friends who watched at his bedside. His last hours were cheered by the presence of an affectionate son; and he died surrounded by friends who, during his long illness, had done all that affection could suggest to soothe his sufferings.

Although this sad event has been expected for many weeks, the shock it produced, and the innumerable tributes of respect to his memory exhibited on every side, and in every form, prove the depth of the public sorrow, and the greatness of the public loss.

Imperishably associated as his name has been for fifty years with every great event affecting the fortunes of our country, it is difficult to realize that he is indeed gone for ever. It is difficult to feel that we shall see no more his noble form within these walls —that we shall hear no more his patriot tones, now rousing his countrymen to vindicate their rights against a foreign foe, now imploring them to preserve concord among themselves. We shall see him no more. The memory and the fruits of his services alone remain to us. Amidst the general gloom, the Capitol itself looks desolate, as if the genius of the place had departed. Already the intelligence has reached almost every quarter of the Republic, and a great people mourn with us, to-day, the death of their most illustrious citizen. Sympathizing, as we do, deeply, with his family and friends, yet private affliction is absorbed in the general sorrow. The spectacle of a whole community lamenting the loss of a great man, is far more touching than any manifestation of private grief. In speaking of a loss which is national, I will not attempt to describe the universal burst of grief with which Kentucky will receive these tidings. The attempt would be vain to depict the gloom that will cover her people, when they know that the pillar of fire is removed, which has guided their footsteps for the life of a generation.

It is known to the country, that from the memorable session of 1849–'50, Mr. CLAY'S health gradually declined. Although several years of his Senatorial term remained, he did not propose to continue in the public service longer than the present session. He came to Washington chiefly to defend, if it should become necessary, the measures of adjustment, to the adoption of which he so largely contributed; but the condition of his health did not allow him, at any time, to participate in the discussions of the Senate. Through the winter, he was confined almost wholly to his room, with slight changes in his condition, but gradually losing the remnant of his strength. Through the long and dreary winter, he conversed much and cheerfully with his friends, and expressed a deep interest in public affairs. Although he did not expect a restoration to health, he cherished the hope that the mild season of spring would bring to him strength enough to return to Ashland, and die in the bosom of his family. But, alas! spring, that brings life to all nature, brought no life nor hope to him. After the month of March, his vital powers rapidly wasted, and for weeks he lay patiently awaiting the stroke of death. But the approach of the destroyer had no terrors for him. No clouds overhung his future. He met the end with composure, and his pathway to the grave was brightened by the immortal hopes which spring from the Christian faith.

Not long before his death, having just returned from Kentucky, I bore to him a token of affection from his excellent wife. Never can I forget his appearance, his manner, or his words. After speaking of his family, his friends, and his country, he changed the conversation to his own future, and looking on me with his fine eye undimmed, and his voice full of its original compass and melody, he said, "I am not afraid to die, sir. I have hope, faith, and some confidence. I do not think any man can be entirely certain in regard to his future state, but I have an abiding trust in the merits and mediation of our Saviour." It will assuage the grief of his family to know that he looked hopefully beyond the tomb, and a Christian people will rejoice to hear that such a man, in his last hours, reposed with simplicity and confidence upon the promises of the Gospel.

It is the custom, on occasions like this, to speak of the parentage and childhood of the deceased, and to follow him, step by step, through life. I will not attempt to relate even all the great events of Mr. CLAY'S life, because they are familiar to the whole country, and it would be needless to enumerate a long list of public services which form a part of American history.

Beginning life as a friendless boy, with few advantages save those conferred by nature, while yet a minor, he left Virginia, the State of his birth, and commenced the practice of law at Lexington, in Kentucky. At a bar remarkable for its numbers and talent, Mr. CLAY soon rose to the first rank. At a very early age he was elected from the county of Fayette to the General Assembly of Kentucky, and was the Speaker of that body. Coming into the Senate of the United States, for the first time, in 1806, he entered upon a parliamentary career, the most brilliant and successful in our annals. From that time he remained habitually in the public eye. As a Senator, as a member of this House and its Speaker, as a representative of his country abroad, and as a high officer in the Executive department of the Government, he was intimately connected for fifty years with every great measure of American policy. Of the mere party measures of this period, I do not propose to speak. Many of them have passed away, and are remembered only as the occasions for the great intellectual efforts which marked their discussion. Concerning others, opinions are still divided. They will go into history, with the reasons on either side rendered by the greatest intellects of the time.

As a leader in a deliberative body, Mr. CLAY had no equal in America. In him, intellect, person, eloquence, and courage, united to form a character fit to command. He fired with his own enthusiasm, and controlled by his amazing will, individuals and masses. No reverse could crush his spirit, nor defeat reduce him to despair. Equally erect and dauntless in prosperity and adversity, when successful, he moved to the accomplishment of his purposes with severe resolution; when defeated, he rallied his broken bands around him, and from his eagle eye shot along their ranks the contagion of his own courage. Destined for a leader, he everywhere asserted his destiny. In his long and eventful life he came in contact with men of all ranks and professions, but he never felt that he was in the presence of a man superior to himself. In the assemblies of the people, at the bar, in the Senate—everywhere within the circle of his personal presence he assumed and maintained a position of preëminence.

But the supremacy of Mr. Clay, as a party leader, was not his only, nor his highest title to renown. That title is to be found in the purely patriotic spirit which, on great occasions, always signalized his conduct. We have had no statesman, who, in periods of real and imminent public peril, has exhibited a more genuine and enlarged patriotism than Henry Clay. Whenever a question presented itself actually threatening the existence of the Union, Mr. Clay, rising above the passions of the hour, always exerted his powers to solve it peacefully and honourably. Although more liable than most men, from his impetuous and ardent nature, to feel strongly the passions common to us all, it was his rare faculty to be able to subdue them in a great crisis, and to hold toward all sections of the confederacy the language of concord and brotherhood.

Sir, it will be a proud pleasure to every true American heart to remember the great occasions when Mr. Clay has displayed a sublime patriotism—when the ill-temper engendered by the times, and the miserable jealousies of the day, seemed to have been driven from his bosom by the expulsive power of nobler feelings—when every throb of his heart was given to his country, every effort of his intellect dedicated to her service. Who does not remember the three periods when the American system of Government was exposed to its severest trials; and who does not know that when history shall relate the struggle which preceded, and the dangers which were averted by the Missouri compromise, the Tariff compromise of 1832, and the adjustment of 1850, the same pages will record the genius, the eloquence, and the patriotism of HENRY CLAY?

Nor was it in Mr. CLAY'S nature to lag behind until measures of adjustment were matured, and then come forward to swell a majority. On the contrary, like a bold and real statesman, he was ever among the first to meet the peril, and hazard his fame upon the remedy. It is fresh in the memory of us all that, when lately the fury of sectional discord threatened to sever the confederacy, Mr. CLAY, though withdrawn from public life, and oppressed by the burden of years, came back to the Senate—the theatre of his glory—and devoted the remnant of his strength to the sacred duty of preserving the union of the States.

With characteristic courage he took the lead in proposing a scheme of settlement. But while he was willing to assume the responsibility of proposing a plan, he did not, with petty ambition, insist upon its adoption to the exclusion of other modes; but, taking his own as a starting point for discussion and practical action, he nobly laboured with his compatriots to change and improve it in such form as to make it an acceptable adjustment. Throughout the long and arduous struggle, the love of country expelled from his bosom the spirit of selfishness, and Mr. CLAY proved, for the third time, that though he was ambitious and loved glory, he had no ambition to mount to fame on the confusions of his country. And this conviction is lodged in the hearts of the people; the party measures and the party passions of former times have not, for several years, interposed between Mr. CLAY and the masses of his countrymen. After 1850, he seemed to feel that his mission was accomplished; and, during the same period, the regards and affections of the American people have been attracted to him in a remarkable degree. For many months, the warmest feelings, the deepest anxieties of all parties, centered upon the dying statesman; the glory of his great actions shed a mellow lustre on his declining years; and to fill the measure of his fame, his countrymen, weaving for him the laurel wreath, with common hands, did bind it about his venerable brows, and send him crowned, to history.

The life of Mr. CLAY, sir, is a striking example of the abiding fame which surely awaits the direct and candid statesman. The entire absence of equivocation or disguise, in all his acts, was his master-key to the popular heart; for while the people will forgive the errors of a bold and open nature, he sins past forgiveness, who deliberately deceives them. Hence Mr. Clay, though often defeated in his measures of policy, always secured the respect of his opponents without losing the confidence of his friends. He never paltered in a double sense. The country was never in doubt as to his opinions or his purposes. In all the contests of his time, his position on great public questions, was as clear as the sun in a cloudless sky. Sir, standing by the grave of this great man, and considering these things, how contemptible does appear the mere legerdemain of politics! What a reproach is his life on that false policy which would trifle with a great and upright people! If I were to write his epitaph, I would inscribe, as the highest eulogy, on the stone which shall mark his resting-place, "Here lies a man who was in the public service for fifty years, and never attempted to deceive his countrymen."

While the youth of America should imitate his noble qualities, they may take courage from his career, and note the high proof it affords that, under our equal institutions, the avenues to honour are open to all. Mr. Clay rose by the force of his own genius, unaided by power, patronage, or wealth. At an age when our young men are usually advanced to the higher schools of learning, provided only with the rudiments of an English education, he turned his steps to the West, and amidst the rude collisions of a border-life, matured a character whose highest exhibitions were destined to mark eras in his country's history. Beginning on the frontiers of American civilization, the orphan boy, supported only by the consciousness of his own powers, and by the confidence of the people, surmounted all the barriers of adverse fortune, and won a glorious name in the annals of his country. Let the generous youth, fired with honourable ambition, remember that the American system of government offers on every hand bounties to merit. If, like CLAY, orphanage, obscurity, poverty, shall oppress him; yet if, like CLAY, he feels the Promethean spark within, let him remember that his country, like a generous mother, extends her arms to welcome and to cherish every one of her children whose genius and worth may promote her prosperity or increase her renown.

Mr. Speaker, the signs of woe around us, and the general voice, announce that another great man has fallen. Our consolation is that he was not taken in the vigour of his manhood, but sank into the grave at the close of a long and illustrious career. The great statesmen who have filled the largest space in the public eye, one by one are passing away. Of the three great leaders of the Senate, one alone remains, and he must follow soon. We shall witness no more their intellectual struggles in the American

Forum; but the monuments of their genius will be cherished as the common property of the people, and their names will continue to confer dignity and renown upon their country.

Not less illustrious than the greatest of these will be the name of CLAY—a name pronounced with pride by Americans in every quarter of the globe; a name to be remembered while history shall record the struggles of modern Greece for freedom, or the spirit of liberty burn in the South American bosom; a living and immortal name—a name that would descend to posterity without the aid of letters, borne by tradition from generation to generation. Every memorial of such a man will possess a meaning and a value to his countrymen. His tomb will be a hallowed spot. Great memories will cluster there, and his countrymen, as they visit it, may well exclaim—

"Such graves as his are pilgrim shrines,
Shrines to no creed or code confined;
The Delphian vales, the Palestines,
The Meccas of the mind."

Mr. Speaker, I offer the following resolutions:

Resolved, That the House of Representatives of the United States has received, with the deepest sensibility, intelligence of the death of HENRY CLAY.

Resolved, That the officers and members of the House of Representatives will wear the usual badge of mourning for thirty days, as a testimony of the profound respect this House entertains for the memory of the deceased.

Resolved, That the officers and members of the House of Representatives, in a body, will attend the funeral of HENRY CLAY, on the day appointed for that purpose by the Senate of the United States.

Resolved, That the proceedings of this House, in relation to the death of HENRY CLAY, be communicated to the family of the deceased by the Clerk.

Resolved, That as a further mark of respect for the memory of the deceased, this House do now adjourn.

Mr. EWING rose and said:

A noble heart has ceased to beat for ever. A long life of brilliant and self-devoted public service is finished at last. We now stand at its conclusion looking back through the changeful history of that life to its beginning, contemporaneous with the very birth of the Republic, and its varied events mingle, in our hearts and our memories, with the triumphs and calamities, the weakness and the power, the adversity and prosperity of a country we love so much. As we contemplate this sad event, in this place, the shadows of the past gather over us; the memories of events long gone crowd upon us, and the shades of departed patriots seem to hover about us, and wait to receive into their midst the spirit of one who was worthy to be a colabourer with them in a common cause, and to share in the rewards of their virtues. Henceforth he must be to us as one of them.

They say he was ambitious. If so, it was a grievous fault, and grievously has he answered it. He has found in it naught but disappointment. It has but served to aggravate the mortification of his defeats, and furnish an additional lustre to the triumph of his foes. Those who come after us may, ay, they will, inquire why his statue stands not among the statues of those whom men thought ablest and worthiest to govern.

But his ambition was a high and holy feeling, unselfish, magnanimous. Its aspirations were for his country's good, and its triumph was his country's prosperity. Whether in honour or reproach, in triumph or defeat, that heart of his never throbbed with one pulsation save for her honour and her welfare. Turn to him in that last best deed, and crowning glory of a life so full of public service and of honour, when his career of personal ambition was finished for ever. Rejected again and again by his countrymen; just abandoned by a party which would scarce have had an existence without his genius, his courage, and his labours, that great heart, ever firm and defiant to the assaults of his enemies, but defenceless against the ingratitude of friends, doubtless wrung with the bitterest mortification of his life—then it was, and under such circumstances as these, the gathering storm rose upon his country. All eyes turned to him; all voices called for those services which, in the hour of prosperity and security, they had so carelessly rejected. With no misanthropic chagrin; with no morose, selfish resentment, he forgot all but his country and that country endangered. He returns to the scene of his labours and his fame which he had thought to have left for ever. A scene—that American Senate Chamber—clothed in no gorgeous drapery, shrouded in no superstitious awe or ancient reverence .for hereditary power, but to a reflecting American mind more full of interest, or dignity, and of grandeur than any spot on this broad earth, not made holy by religion's consecrating seal. See him as he enters there, tremblingly, but hopefully, upon the last, most momentous, perhaps most doubtful conflict of his life. Sir, many a gay tournament has been more dazzling to the eye of fancy, more gorgeous and imposing in the display of jewelry and cloth of gold, in the sound of heralds' trumpets, in the grand array of princely beauty and of royal pride. Many a battle-field has trembled beneath a more ostentatious parade of human power, and its conquerors have been crowned with laurels, honoured with triumphs, and apotheosised amid the demigods of history; but to the thoughtful, hopeful, philanthropic student of the annals of his race, never was there a conflict in which such dangers were threatened, such hopes imperiled, or the hero of which deserved a warmer gratitude, a nobler triumph, or a prouder monument.

Sir, from that long, anxious, and exhausting conflict, he never rose again. In that last battle for his country's honour and his country's safety, he received the mortal wound which laid him low, and we now mourn the death of a martyred patriot.

But never, in all the grand drama which the story of his life arrays, never has he presented a sublimer or a more touching spectacle than in those last days of his decline and death. Broken with the storms of State, wounded and scathed in many a fiery conflict, that aged, worn, and decayed body, in such mournful contrast with the never-dying strength of his giant spirit, he seemed a proud and sacred, though a crumbling monument of past glory. Standing among us, like some ancient colossal ruin amid the degenerate and more diminutive structures of modern times, its vast proportions magnified by the contrast, he reminded us of those days when there were giants in the land, and we remembered that even then there was none whose prowess could withstand his arm. To watch him in that slow decline, yielding with dignity, and as it were inch by inch, to that last enemy, as a hero yields to a conquering foe, the glorious light of his intellect blazing still in all its wonted brilliancy, and setting at defiance the clouds that vainly attempted to obscure it, he was more full of interest than in the day of his glory and his power. There are some men whose brightest intellectual emanations rise so little superior to the instincts of the animal, that we are led fearfully to doubt that cherished truth of the soul's immortality, which, even in despair, men press to their doubting hearts. But it is in the death of such a man as he that we are reassured by the contemplation, of a kindred, though superior spirit, of a soul which, immortal, like his fame, knows no old age, no decay, no death.

The wondrous light of his unmatched intellect may have dazzled a world; the eloquence of that inspired tongue may have enchanted millions, but there are few who have sounded the depths of that noble heart. To see him in sickness and in health, in joy and in sadness, in the silent watches of the night and in the busy daytime—this it was to know and love him. To see the impetuous torrent of that resistless will; the hurricane of those passions hushed in peace, breathe calm and gently as a summer zephyr; to feel the gentle pressure of that hand in the grasp of friendship which in the rage of fiery conflict would hurl scorn and defiance at his foe; to see that eagle eye which oft would burn with patriotic ardour, or flash with the lightning of his anger, beam with the kindliest expressions of tenderness and affection—then it was, and then alone, we could learn to know and feel that that heart was warmed by the same sacred fire from above which enkindled the light of his resplendent intellect. In the death of such a man even patriotism itself might pause, and for a moment stand aloof while friendship shed a tear of sorrow upon his bier.

> "His life was gentle; and the elements
> So mix'd in him, that Nature might stand up
> And say to all the world, *This was a man!*"

But who can estimate his country's loss? What tongue portray the desolation which in this hour throughout this broad land hangs like a gloomy pall over his grief-stricken countrymen? How poorly can words like mine translate the eloquence of a whole people's grief for a patriot's death. For a nation's loss let a nation mourn. For that stupendous calamity to our country and mankind, be the heavens hung with black; let the wailing elements chant his dirge, and the universal heart of man throb with one common pang of grief and anguish.

Mr. CASKIE said:—

Mr. SPEAKER: Unwell as I am, I must try to lay a single laurel leaf in that open coffin which is already garlanded by the eloquent tributes to the illustrious Departed, which have been heard in this now solemn Hall; for I come, sir, from the district of his birth. I represent on this floor that old Hanover so proud of her Henrys—her Patrick Henry and her HENRY CLAY. I speak for a People among whom he has always had as earnest and devoted friends as were ever the grace and glory of a patriot and statesman.

I shall attempt no sketch of his life. That you have had from other and abler hands than mine. Till yesterday that life was, of his own free gift, the property of his country; to-day it belongs to her history. It is known to all, and will not be forgotten. Constant, stern opponent of his political school as has been my State, I say for her, that nowhere in this broad land are his great qualities more admired, or is his death more mourned, than in Virginia. Well may this be so; for she is his mother, and he was her son.

Mr. Speaker, when I remember the party strifes in which he was so much mingled, and through which we all more or less have passed, and then survey this scene, and think how far, as the lightning has borne the news that he is gone, half-masted flags are drooping and church bells are tolling, and hearts are sorrowing, I can but feel that it is good for man to die. For when Death enters, O! how the unkindnesses, and jealousies, and rivalries of life do vanish, and how like incense from an altar do peace, and friendship, and all the sweet charities of our nature, rise around the corpse which was once a man! And of a truth, Mr. Speaker, never was more of veritable noble *manhood* cased in mortal mould than was found in him to whose memory this brief and humble, yet true and heartfelt tribute is paid. But his eloquent voice is hushed, his high heart is stilled. "Like a shock of corn fully ripe, he has been gathered to his fathers." With more than three score years and ten upon him, and honours clustered thick about him, in the full possession of unclouded intellect, and all the consolations of Christianity, he has met the fate which is evitable by none. Lamented by all his countrymen, his name is bright on Fame's immortal roll. He has finished his course, and he has his crown. What more fruit can life bear? What can it give that HENRY CLAY has not gained?

Then, Mr. Speaker, around his tomb should be heard not only the dirge that wails his loss, but the jubilant anthem which sounds that on the world's battle-field another victory has been won—another *incontestable greatness* achieved.

Mr. CHANDLER, of Pennsylvania, said:—

Mr. SPEAKER: It would seem as if the solemn invocation of the honourable gentleman from Kentucky (Mr. EWING) was receiving an early answer, and that the heavens are hung in black, and the wailing elements are singing the funeral dirge of HENRY CLAY. Amid this elemental gloom, and the distress which pervades the nation at the death of HENRY CLAY, private grief should not obtrude itself upon notice, nor personal anguish seek for utterance. Silence is the best exponent of individual sorrow, and the heart that knoweth its own bitterness shrinks from an exposition of its affliction.

Could I have consulted my own feelings on the event which occupies the attention of the House at the present moment, I should even have forborne attendance here, and in the solitude and silence of my chamber have mused upon the terrible lesson which has been administered to the people and the nation. But I represent a constituency who justly pride themselves upon the unwavering attachment they have ever felt and manifested to Henry Clay—a constant, pervading, hereditary love. The son has taken up the father's affection, and amid all the professions of political attachments to others, whom the accidents of party have made prominent, and the success of party has made powerful, true to his own instincts, and true to the sanctified legacy of his father, he has placed the name of Henry Clay forward and pre-eminent as the exponent of what is greatest in statesmanship and purest in patriotism. And even, sir, when party fealty caused other attachments to be avowed for party uses, the preference was limited to the occupancy of office, and superiority admitted for Clay in all that is reckoned above party estimation.

Nor ought I to forbear to add that, as the senior member of the delegation which represents my Commonwealth, I am requested to utter the sentiments of the people of Pennsylvania at large, who yield to no portion of this great Union in their appreciation of the talents, their reverence for the lofty patriotism, their admiration of the statesmanship, and hereafter their love of the memory of HENRY CLAY.

I cannot, therefore, be silent on this occasion without injustice to the affections of my constituency, even though I painfully feel how inadequate to the reverence and love my people have toward that statesman must be all that I have to utter on this mournful occasion.

I know not, Mr. Chairman, where now the nation is to find the men she needs in peril; either other calls than those of politics are holding in abeyance the talents which the nation may need, or else a generation is to pass undistinguished by the greatness of our statesmen. Of the noble minds that have swayed the Senate one yet survives in the maturity of powerful intellect, carefully disciplined and nobly exercised. May He who has thus far blessed our nation, spare to her and the world that of which the world must always envy our country the possession! But my business is with the dead.

The biography of HENRY CLAY, from his childhood upward, is too familiar to every American for me to trespass on the time of this House by a reference directly thereto; and the honourable gentlemen who have preceded me have, with affectionate hand and appropriate delicacy, swept away the dust which nearly fourscore years have scattered over a part of the record, and have made our pride greater in his life, and our grief more poignant at his death, by showing some of those passages which attract respect to our republican institutions, of which Mr. CLAY'S whole life was the able support and the most successful illustration.

It would, then, be a work of supererogation for me to renew that effort, though inquiry into the life and conduct of HENRY CLAY would present new themes for private eulogy, new grounds for public gratitude.

How rare is it, Mr. Speaker, that the great man, living, can with confidence rely on extensive personal friendship, or dying, think to awaken a sentiment of regret beyond that which includes the public loss or the disappointment of individual hopes. Yet, sir, the message which yesterday went forth from this city that HENRY CLAY was dead, brought sorrow, personal, private, special sorrow, to the hearts of thousands; each of whom felt that from his own love for, his long attachment to, his disinterested hopes in HENRY CLAY, he had a particular sorrow to cherish and express, which weighed upon his heart separate from the sense of national loss.

No man, Mr. Speaker, in our nation had the art so to identify himself with public measures of the most momentous character, and to maintain at the same time almost universal affection, like that great statesman. His business, from his boyhood, was with national concerns, and he dealt with them as with familiar things. And yet his sympathies were with individual interests, enterprises, affections, joys, and sorrows; and while every patriot bowed in humble deference to his lofty attainments and heart-felt gratitude for his national services, almost every man in this vast Republic knew that the great statesman was, in feeling and experience, identified with his own position. Hence the universal love of the people; hence their enthusiasm in all times for his fame. Hence, sir, their present grief.

Many other public men of our country have distinguished themselves and brought honour to the nation by superiority in some peculiar branch of public service, but it seems to have been the gift of Mr. Clay to have acquired peculiar eminence in every path of duty he was called to tread. In the earnestness of debate, which great public interests and distinguished opposing talents excited in this House, he had no superior in energy, force, or effect. Yet, as the presiding officer, by blandness of language and firmness of purpose, he soothed and made orderly; and thus, by official dignity, he commanded the respect which energy had secured to him on the floor.

Wherever official or social duties demanded an exercise of his power there was a pre-eminence which seemed prescriptively his own. In the lofty debate of the Senate and the stirring harangues to popular assemblages, he was the orator of the nation and of the people; and the sincerity of purpose and the unity of design evinced in all he said or did, fixed in the public mind a confidence strong and expansive as the affections he had won.

Year after year, sir, has HENRY CLAY been achieving the work of the mission with which he was intrusted; and it was only when the warmest wishes of his warmest friends were disappointed, that he entered on the fruition of a patriot's highest hopes, and stood in the full enjoyment of that admiration and confidence which nothing but the antagonism of party relations could have divided.

How rich that enjoyment must have been it is only for us to imagine. How eminently deserved it was we and the world can attest.

The love and the devotion of his political friends were cheering and grateful to his heart, and were acknowledged in all his life—were recognised even to his death.

The contest in the Senate Chamber or the forum were rewarded with success achieved, and the great victor could enjoy the ovation which partial friendship or the gratitude of the benefit prepared. But the triumph of his life was no party achievement. It was not in the applause which admiring friends and defeated antagonists offered to his measureless success, that he found the reward of his labours, and comprehended the extent of his mission.

It was only when friends and antagonists paused in their contests, appalled at the public difficulties and national dangers which had been accumulating, unseen and unregarded; it was only when the nation itself felt the danger, and acknowledged the inefficacy of party action as a remedy, that Henry Clay calculated the full extent of his powers, and enjoyed the reward of their saving exercise. Then, sir, you saw, and I saw, party designations dropped, and party allegiance disavowed, and anxious patriots, of all localities and name, turn toward the country's benefactor as the man for the terrible exigencies of the hour; and the sick chamber of Henry Clay became the Delphos whence were given out the oracles that presented the means and the measures of our Union's safety. There, sir, and not in the high places of the country, were the labours and sacrifices of half a century to be rewarded and closed. With his right yet in that Senate which he had entered the youngest, and lingered still the eldest member, he felt that his work was done, and the object of his life accomplished. Every cloud that had dimmed the noonday lustre had been dissipated; and the retiring orb, which sunk from the sight of the nation in fullness and in beauty, will yet pour up the horizon a posthumous glory that shall tell of the splendour and greatness of the luminary that has passed away.

Mr. BAYLY, of Virginia.

Mr. SPEAKER: Although I have been all my life a political opponent of Mr. CLAY, yet from my boyhood I have been upon terms of personal friendship with him. More than twenty years ago, I was introduced to him by my father, who was his personal friend. From that time to this, there has existed between us as great personal intimacy as the disparity in our years and our political difference would justify. After I became a member of this House, and upon his return to the Senate, subsequent to his resignation in 1842, the warm regard upon his part for the daughter of a devoted friend of forty years' standing, made him a constant visitor at my house, and frequently a guest at my table. These circumstances make it proper, that upon this occasion, I should pay this last tribute to his memory. I not only knew him well as a statesman, but I knew him better in most unreserved social intercourse. The most happy circumstance, as I esteem it, of my political life has been, that I have thus known each of our great Congressional triumvirate.

I, sir, never knew a man of higher qualities than Mr. CLAY. His very faults originated in high qualities. With as great self-possession, with greater self-reliance than any man I ever knew, he possessed moral and physical courage to as high a degree as any man who ever lived. Confident in his own judgment, never doubting as to his own course, fearing no obstacle that might lie in his way, it was almost impossible that he should not have been imperious in his character. Never doubting himself as to what, in his opinion, duty and patriotism required at his hands, it was natural that he should sometimes have been impatient with those more doubting and timid than himself. His were qualities to have made a great general, as they were qualities that did make him a great statesman, and these qualities were so obvious that during the darkest period of our late war with Great Britain, Mr. Madison had determined, at one time, to make him General-in-Chief of the American army.

Sir, it is but a short time since the American Congress buried the first one that went to the grave of that great triumvirate. We are now called upon to bury another. The third, thank God! still lives, and long may he live to enlighten his countrymen by his wisdom, and set them the example of exalted patriotism. Sir, in the lives and characters of these great men, there is much resembling those of the great triumvirate of the British Parliament. It differs principally in this: Burke preceded Fox and Pitt to the tomb. Webster survives Clay and Calhoun. When Fox and Pitt died, they left no peer behind them. Webster still lives, now that Calhoun and Clay are dead, the unrivalled statesman of his country. Like Fox and Pitt, Clay and Calhoun lived in troubled times. Like Fox and

Pitt they were each of them the leader of rival parties. Like Fox and Pitt they were idolized by their respective friends. Like Fox and Pitt, they died about the same time, and in the public service; and as has been said of Fox and Pitt, Clay and Calhoun died with "their harness upon them." Like Fox and Pitt—

"With more than mortal powers endow'd
How high they soar'd above the crowd;
Theirs was no common party race,
Jostling by dark intrigue for place—
Like fabled gods their mighty war
Shook realms and nations in its jar.
Beneath each banner proud to stand,
Look'd up the noblest of the land.
* * * * *
Here let their discord with them die.
Speak not for those a separate doom;
Whom fate made brothers in the tomb;
But search the land of living men,
Where wilt thou find their like again?"

Mr. VENABLE, said:—

Mr. SPEAKER: I trust that I shall be pardoned for adding a few words upon this sad occasion. The life of the illustrious statesman which has just terminated is so interwoven with our history, and the lustre of his great name so profusely shed over its pages, that simple admiration of his high qualities might well be my excuse. But it is a sacred privilege to draw near; to contemplate the end of the great and the good. It is profitable as well as purifying to look upon and realize the office of death in removing all that can excite jealousy or produce distrust, and to gaze upon the virtues which, like jewels, have survived his powers of destruction. The light which radiates from the life of a great and patriotic statesman is often dimmed by the mists which party conflicts throw around it. But the blast which strikes him down purifies the atmosphere which surrounded him in life, and it shines forth in bright examples and well-earned renown. It is then that we witness the sincere acknowledgment of gratitude by a people who, having enjoyed the benefits arising from the services of an eminent statesman, embalm his name in their memory and hearts. We should cherish such recollections as well from patriotism as self-respect. Ours, sir, is now the duty, in the midst of sadness, in this high place, in the face of our Republic, and before the world, to pay this tribute by acknowledging the merits of our colleague, whose name has ornamented the Journals of Congress for near half a century. Few, very few, have ever combined the high intellectual powers and distinguished gifts of this illustrious Senator. Cast in the finest mould by nature, he more than fulfilled the anticipations which were indulged by those who looked to a distinguished career as the certain result of that zealous pursuit of fame and usefulness upon which he entered in early life. Of the incidents of that life it is unnecessary for me to speak—they are as familiar as household words, and must be equally familiar to those who come after us. But it is useful to refresh memory, by recurrence to some of the events which marked his career. We know, sir, that there is much that is in common in the histories of distinguished men. The elements which constitute greatness are the same in all times; hence those who have been the admiration of their generations present in their lives much which, although really great, ceases to be remarkable, because illustrated by such numerous examples—

> "But there are deeds which should not pass away,
> And names that must not wither."

Of such deeds the life of HENRY CLAY affords many and bright examples. His own name, and those with whom he associated, shall live with a freshness which time cannot impair, and shine with a brightness which passing years cannot dim. His advent into public life was as remarkable for the circumstances as it was brilliant in its effect. It was at a time in which genius and learning, statesmanship and eloquence, made the American Congress the most august body in the world. He was the contemporary of a race of statesmen, some of whom—then administering the Government, and others retiring and retired from office—presented an array of ability unsurpassed in our history. The elder Adams, Jefferson, Madison, Gallatin, Clinton, and Monroe, stood before the Republic in the maturity of their fame; while Calhoun, John Quincy Adams, Lowndes, Randolph, Crawford, Gaston, and

Cheves, with a host of others, rose a bright galaxy upon our horizon. He who won his spurs in such a field earned his knighthood. Distinction amid such competition was true renown—

> "The fame which a man wins for himself is best—
> That he may call his own."

It was such a fame that he made for himself in that most eventful era in our history. To me, sir, the recollections of that day, and the events which distinguish it, is filled with an overpowering interest. I never can forget my enthusiastic admiration of the boldness, the eloquence, and the patriotism of HENRY CLAY during the war of 1812. In the bright array of talent which adorned the Congress of the United States; in the conflict growing out of the political events of that time; in the struggles of party, and amid the gloom and disasters which depressed the spirits of most men, and well nigh paralyzed the energies of the Administration, his cheerful face, high bearing, commanding eloquence and iron will, gave strength and consistency to those elements which finally gave not only success but glory to the country. When dark clouds hovered over us, and there was little to save from despair, the country looked with hope to CLAY and Calhoun, to Lowndes, and Crawford, and Cheves, and looked not in vain. The unbending will, the unshaken nerve, and the burning eloquence of HENRY CLAY did as much to command confidence and sustain hope as even the news of our first victory after a succession of defeats. Those great names are now canonized in history; he, too, has passed to join them on its pages. Associated in his long political life with the illustrious Calhoun, he survived him but two years. Many of us heard his eloquent tribute to his memory in the Senate Chamber on the annunciation of his death. And we this day unite in a similar manifestation of reverential regard to him whose voice shall never more charm the ear, whose burning thoughts, borne on that medium, shall no more move the hearts of listening assemblies.

In the midst of the highest specimens of our race, he was always an equal; *he was a man among men.* Bold, skilful, and determined, he gave character to the party which acknowledged him as a leader; impressed his opinions upon their minds, and an attachment to himself upon their hearts. No man, sir, can do this without being eminently great. Whoever attains this position must first overcome the aspirations of antagonist ambition, quiet the clamours of rivalry, hold in check the murmurs of jealousy, and overcome the instincts of vanity and self-love in the masses thus subdued to his control. But few men ever attain it. Very rare are the examples of those whose plastic touch forms the minds and directs the purposes of a great political party. This infallible indication of superiority belonged to Mr. Clay. He has exercised that control during a long life; and now through our broad land the tidings of his death, borne with electric speed, have opened the fountains of sorrow. Every city, town, village, and hamlet will be clothed with mourning; along our extended coast, the commercial and military marine, with flags drooping at half-mast, own the bereavement; State-houses draped in black proclaim the extinguishment of one of the great lights of Senates; and minute-guns sound his requiem!

Sir, during the last five years I have seen the venerable John Quincy Adams, John C. Calhoun, and HENRY CLAY pass from among us, the legislators of our country. The race of giants who "were on the earth in those days" is well-nigh gone. Despite their skill, their genius, their might, they have sunk under the stroke of time. They were our admiration and our glory; a few linger with us, the monuments of former greatness, the beacon-lights of a past age. The death of HENRY CLAY cannot fail to suggest melancholy associations to each member of this House. These walls have re-echoed the silvery tones of his bewitching voice; listening assemblies have hung upon his lips. The chair which you fill has been graced by his presence, while his commanding person and unequalled parliamentary attainments inspired all with deference and respect. Chosen by acclamation because of his high qualifications, he sustained himself before the House and the country. In his supremacy with his party, and the uninterrupted confidence which he enjoyed to the day of his death, he seems to have almost discredited the truth of those lines of the poet Laberius—

> "Non possunt primi esse omnes omni in tempore,
> Summum ad gradum cum claritatis veneris,
> Consistes ægre, et citius, quam ascendas, cades."

If not at all times first, he stood equal with the foremost, and a brilliant rapid rise knew no decline in the confidence of those whose just appreciation of his merits had confirmed his title to renown.

The citizens of other countries will deplore his death; the struggling patriots who on our own continent were cheered by his sympathies, and who must have perceived his influence in the recognition of their independence by this Government, have taught their children to venerate his name. He won the civic crown, and the demonstrations of this hour own the worth of civil services.

It was with great satisfaction that I heard my friend from Kentucky, [Mr. BRECKENRIDGE,] the immediate representative of Mr. CLAY, detail a conversation which disclosed the feelings of that eminent man in relation to his Christian hope. These, Mr. Speaker, are rich memorials, precious reminiscences. A Christian statesman is the glory of his age, and his memory will be glorious in after times; it reflects a light coming from a source which clouds cannot dim nor shadows obscure. It was my privilege, also, a short time since, to converse with this distinguished statesman on the subject of his hopes in a future state. Feeling a deep interest, I asked him frankly what were his hopes in the world to which he was evidently hastening. "I am pleased," said he, "my friend, that you have introduced the subject. Conscious that I must die very soon, I love to meditate upon the most important of all interests. I love to converse and to hear conversations about them. The vanity of the world and its insufficiency to satisfy the soul of man has long been a settled conviction of my mind. Man's inability to secure by his own merits the approbation of God, I feel to be true. I trust in the atonement of the Saviour of men as the ground of my acceptance and my hope of salvation. My faith is feeble, but I hope in His mercy and trust in His promises." To such declarations I listened with the deepest interest, as I did on another occasion, when he said: "I am willing to abide the will of Heaven, and ready to die when that will shall determine it."

He is gone, sir, professing the humble hope of a Christian. That hope, alone, sir, can sustain you, or any of us. There is one lonely and crushed heart that has bowed before this afflictive event. Far away, at Ashland, a widowed wife, prevented by feeble health from attending his bedside and soothing his painful hours, she has thought even the electric speed of the intelligence daily transmitted of his condition too slow for her aching, anxious bosom.

She will find consolation in his Christian submission, and will draw all of comfort that such a case admits from the assurance that nothing was neglected by the kindness of friends which could supply her place. May the guardianship of the widow's God be her protection, and His consolations her support!

> "All cannot be at all times first,
> To reach the topmost step of glory; to stand there
> More hard. Even swifter than we mount we fall."

Mr. HAVEN, said:—

Mr. SPEAKER: Representing a constituency distinguished for the constancy of its devotion to the political principles of Mr. CLAY, and for its unwavering attachment to his fortunes and his person—sympathizing deeply with those whose more intimate personal relations with him have made them feel most profoundly this general bereavement—I desire to say a few words of him, since he has fallen amongst us, and been taken to his rest.

After the finished eulogies which have been so eloquently pronounced by the honourable gentlemen who have preceded me, I will avoid a course of remark which might otherwise be deemed a repetition, and refer to the bearing of some of the acts of the deceased upon the interests and destinies of my own State. The influence of his public life, and of his *purely American character*, the benefits of his wise forecast, and the results of his efforts for wholesome and rational progress, are nowhere more strongly exhibited than in the State of New York.

Our appreciation of his anxiety for the general diffusion of knowledge and education, is manifested in our twelve thousand public libraries, our equal number of common schools, and a large number of higher institutions of learning, all of which draw portions of their support from the share of the proceeds of the public lands, which his wise policy gave to our State. Our whole people are thus constantly reminded of their great obligations to the statesman whose death now afflicts the nation with sorrow. Our extensive public works, attest our conviction of the utility and importance of the system of internal improvements he so ably advocated; and their value and productiveness, afford a most striking evidence of the soundness and wisdom of his policy. Nor has his influence been less sensibly felt in our agriculture, commerce, and manufactures. Every department of human industry acknowledges his fostering care; and the people of New York are, in no small measure, indebted to his statesmanship for the wealth, comfort, contentment, and happiness so widely and generally diffused throughout the State.

Well may New York cherish his memory and acknowlege with gratitude the benefits that his life has conferred. That memory will be cherished throughout the Republic.

When internal discord and sectional strife have

threatened the integrity of the Union, his just weight of character, his large experience, his powers of conciliation and acknowledged patriotism, have enabled him to pacify the angry passions of his countrymen, and to raise the bow of promise and of hope upon the clouds which have darkened the political horizon.

He has passed from amongst us, ripe in wisdom and pure in character—full of years and full of honours—he has breathed his last amidst the blessings of a united and grateful nation.

He was, in my judgment, particularly fortunate in the time of his death.

He lived to see his country, guided by his wisdom, come once again unhurt, out of trying sectional difficulties and domestic strife; and he has closed his eyes in death upon that country, whilst it is in the enjoyment of profound peace, busy with industry, and blessed with unequalled prosperity.

It can fall to the lot of but few to die amidst so warm a gratitude flowing from the hearts of their countrymen; and none can leave a brighter example or a more enduring fame.

Mr. Brooks, of New York, said:—

Mr. Speaker: I rise to add my humble tribute to the memory of a great and good man now to be gathered to his fathers. I speak for, and from, a community in whose heart is enshrined the name of him whom we mourn; who, however much Virginia, the land of his birth, or Kentucky, the land of his adoption, may love him, is, if possible, loved where I live yet more. If idolatry had been Christian, or allowable even, he would have been our idol. But as it is, for a quarter of a century now, his bust, his portrait, or some medal, has been one of our household gods, gracing not alone the saloons and the halls of wealth, but the humblest room or workshop of almost every mechanic or labourer. Proud monuments of his policy as a statesman, as my colleague has justly said, are all about us; and we owe to him, in a good degree, our growth, our greatness, our prosperity and happiness as a people.

The great field of Henry Clay, Mr. Speaker, has been here, on the floor of this House, and in the other wing of the Capitol. He has held other posts of higher nominal distinction, but they are all eclipsed by the brilliancy of his career as a Congressman. What of glory he has acquired, or what most endear him to his countrymen, have been won, here, amid these pillars, under these domes of the Capitol.

"Si quæris monumentum, circumspice."

The mind of Mr. Clay has been the governing mind of the country, more or less, ever since he has been on the stage of public action. In a minority or majority—more, perhaps, even in a minority than in a majority—he seems to have had some commission, divine as it were, to persuade, to convince, to govern other men. His patriotism, his grand conceptions, have created measures which the secret fascination of his manners, in-doors, or his irresistible eloquence without, have enabled him almost always to frame into laws. Adverse administrations have yielded to him, or been borne down by him, or he has taken them captive as a leader, and carried the country and Congress with him. This power he has wielded now for nearly half a century, with nothing but Reason and Eloquence to back him. And yet when he came here, years ago, he came from a then frontier State of this Union, heralded by no loud trumpet of fame, nay, quite unknown! unfortified even by any position, social or pecuniary;—to quote his own words, "My only heritage has been infancy, indigence, and ignorance."

In these days, Mr. Speaker, when mere civil qualifications for high public places—when long civil training and practical statesmanship are held subordinate—a most discouraging prospect would be rising up before our young men, were it not for some such names as Lowndes, Crawford, Clinton, Gaston, Calhoun, CLAY, and the like, scattered along the pages of our history, as stars or constellations along a cloudless sky. They shine forth and show us, that if the Chief Magistracy cannot be won by such qualifications, a memory among men can be—a hold upon posterity, as firm, as lustrous—nay, more imperishable. In the Capitolium of Rome there are long rows of marble slabs, on which are recorded the names of the Roman consuls; but the eye wanders over this wilderness of letters but to light up and kindle upon some Cato or Cicero. To win such fame, thus unsullied, as Mr. CLAY has won, is worth any man's ambition. And how was it won? By courting the shifting gales of popularity? No, never! By truckling to the schemes, the arts, and seductions of the demagogue? Never, never! His hardest battles as a public man—his greatest, most illustrious achievements—have been against, at first, an adverse public opinion. To gain an imperishable name, he has often braved the perishable popularity of the moment. That sort of courage which, in a public man, I deem the highest of all courage, that sort of courage most necessary under our form of government to guide as well as to save a State, Mr. CLAY was possessed of more than any public man I ever knew. Physical courage, valuable, indispensable though it be, we share but with the brute; but moral courage, to dare to do right amid all temptations to do wrong, is, as it seems to me, the very highest species, the noblest heroism, under institutions like ours. "I had rather be right than be President," was Mr. CLAY's sublime reply when pressed to refrain from some measure that would mar his popularity. These lofty words were the clue of his whole character—the secret of his hold upon the heads as well as hearts of the American people; nay, the key of his immortality.

Another of the keys, Mr. Speaker, of his universal reputation was his intense nationality. When taunted but recently, almost within our hearing, as it were, on the floor of the Senate by a Southern Senator, as being a Southern man unfaithful to the South—his indignant but patriotic exclamation was, "I know no *South*, no North, no East, no West." The country, the *whole* country, loved, reverenced, adored such a man. The soil of Virginia may be his birthplace, the sod of Kentucky will cover his grave—what was mortal they claim—but the spirit, the soul, the genius of the mighty man, the immortal part, these belong to his country and to his God.

Mr. FAULKNER, of Virginia, said:—

Representing, in part, the State which gave birth to that distinguished man whose death has just been announced upon this floor, and having for many years held toward him the most cordial relations of friendship, personal and political, I feel that I should fail to discharge an appropriate duty, if I permitted this occasion to pass by without some expression of the feeling which such an event is so well calculated to elicit. Sir, this intelligence does not fall upon our ears unexpectedly. For months the public mind has been prepared for the great national loss which we now deplore; and yet, as familiar as the daily and hourly reports have made us with his hopeless condition and gradual decline, and although

> "Like a shadow thrown
> Softly and sweetly from a passing cloud,
> Death fell upon him,"

it is impossible that a light of such surpassing splendour should be, as it is now, for ever extinguished from our view, without producing a shock, deeply and painfully felt, to the utmost limits of this great Republic. Sir, we all feel that a mighty intellect has passed from among us; but, happily for this country, happily for mankind, not until it had accomplished to some extent the exalted mission for which it had been sent upon this earth; not until it had reached the full maturity of its usefulness and power; not until it had shed a bright and radiant lustre over our national renown; not until time had enabled it to bequeath the rich treasures of its thought and experience for the guidance and instruction of the present and of succeeding generations.

Sir, it is difficult,—it is impossible,—within the limit allowed for remarks upon occasions of this kind, to do justice to a great historical character like HENRY CLAY. He was one of that class of men whom Scaliger designates as *homines centenarii*—men that appear upon the earth but once in a century. His fame is the growth of years, and it would require time to unfold the elements which have combined to impart to it so much of stability and grandeur. Volumes have already been written, and volumes will continue to be written, to record those eminent and distinguished public services which have placed him in the front rank of American statesmen and patriots. The highest talents, stimulated by a fervid and patriotic enthusiasm, has already and will continue to exhaust its powers to portray those striking and generous incidents of his life,—those shining and captivating qualities of his heart, which have made him one of the most beloved, as he was one of the most admired, of men; and yet the subject itself will remain as fresh and exhaustless as if hundreds of the best intellects of the land had not quaffed the inspiration of their genius from the ever-gushing and overflowing fountains of his fame. It could not be that a reputation so grand and colossal as that which attaches to the name of HENRY CLAY could rest for its base upon any single virtue, however striking; nor upon any single act, no matter how marked or distinguished. Such a reputation as he has left behind him, could only be the result of a long life of illustrious public service. And such in truth it was. For nearly half a century he has been a prominent actor in all the stirring and eventful scenes of American history, fashioning and moulding many of the most important measures of public policy by his bold and sagacious mind, and arresting others by his unconquerable energy and resistless force of eloquence. And however much the members of this body may differ in opinion as to the wisdom of many of his views of national domestic policy, there is not one upon this floor—no, sir, not one in this nation—who will deny to him frankness and directness as a public man; a genius for statesmanship of the highest order; extraordinary capacities for public usefulness, and an ardent and elevated patriotism, without stain and without reproach.

In referring to a career of public service so varied and extended as that of Mr. CLAY, and to a character so rich in every great and manly virtue, it is only possible to glance at a few of the most prominent of those points of his personal history, which have given to him so distinguished a place in the affections of his countrymen.

In the whole character of Mr. CLAY, in all that attached or belonged to it, you find nothing that is not essentially AMERICAN. Born in the darkest period of our revolutionary struggle; reared from infancy to manhood among those great minds which gave the first impulse to that mighty movement, he early imbibed and sedulously cherished those great principles of civil and political liberty, which he so brilliantly illustrated in his subsequent life, and which has made his name a watchword of hope and consolation to the oppressed of all the earth. In his intellectual training he was the pure creation of our own republican soil. Few, if any, allusions are to be seen in his speeches or writings to ancient or modern literature, or to the thoughts and ideas of other men.

His country, its institutions, its policy, its interests, its destiny, form the exclusive topics of those eloquent harangues which, while they are destitute of the elaborate finish, have all the ardour and intensity of thought; the earnestness of purpose, the cogency of reasoning, the vehemence of style, and the burning patriotism which mark the productions of the great Athenian orator.

One of the most distinguishing characteristics of Mr. CLAY as a public man was his loyalty to truth and to the honest convictions of his own mind. He deceived no man: he would not permit his own heart to be deceived by any of those seductive influences which too often warp the judgment of men in public station. He never paused to consider how far any step which he was about to take would lead to his own personal advancement; he never calculated what he might lose or what he might gain by his advocacy of, or his opposition to, any particular measure. His single inquiry was, Is it right? Is it in accordance with the Constitution of the land? Will it redound to the permanent welfare of the country? When satisfied upon these points, his determination was fixed; his purpose was immovable. "I would rather be right than President" was the expression of his genuine feelings, and the principle by which he was controlled in his public career —a saying worthy of immortality, and proper to be inscribed upon the heart of every young man in this

Republic. And yet, sir, with all of that personal and moral intrepidity which so eminently marked the character of Mr. CLAY; with his well-known inflexibility of purpose and unyielding resolution, such was the genuine sincerity of his patriotism, and such his thorough comprehension of those principles of compromise, upon which the whole structure of our Government was founded, that no one was more prompt to relax the rigour of his policy the moment he perceived that it was calculated to disturb the harmony of the States, or to endanger in any degree the stability of the Government. With him the love of this Union was a passion—an absorbing sentiment—which gave colour to every act of his public life. It triumphed over party; it triumphed over policy; it subdued the natural fierceness and haughtiness of his temper, and brought him into the most kindly and cordial relations with those who, upon all other questions, were deeply and bitterly opposed to him. It has been asserted, sir, upon high medical authority, and doubtless with truth, that his life was in all probability shortened ten years by the arduous and extraordinary labours which he assumed at the memorable session of 1850. If so, he has added the crowning glory of the MARTYR to the spotless fame of the PATRIOT; and we may well hope that a great national pacification, purchased at such a sacrifice, will long continue to cement the bonds of this now happy and prosperous Union.

Mr. Clay possessed, in an eminent degree, the qualities of a great popular leader; and history, I will assume to say, affords no example in any republic, ancient or modern, of any individual that so fearlessly carried out the convictions of his own judgment, and so sparingly flattered the prejudices of popular feeling, who, for so long a period, exercised the same controlling influence over the public mind. Earnest in whatever measure he sustained, fearless in attack,—dexterous in defence,—abounding in intellectual resource,—eloquent in debate,—of inflexible purpose, and with a "courage never to submit or yield," no man ever lived with higher qualifications to rally a desponding party, or to lead an embattled host to victory. That he never attained the highest post of honourable ambition in this country is not to be ascribed to any want of capacity as a popular leader, nor to the absence of those qualities which attract the fidelity and devotion of "troops" of admiring friends. It was the fortune of Napoleon, at a critical period of his destiny, to be brought into collision with the star of Wellington; and it was the fortune of Henry Clay to have encountered, in his political orbit, another great and original mind, gifted with equal power for commanding success, and blessed with more fortunate elements, concurring at the time, of securing popular favour. The struggle was such as might have been anticipated from the collision of two such fierce and powerful rivals. For near a quarter of a century this great republic has been convulsed to its centre by the divisions which have sprung from their respective opinions, policy, and personal destinies; and even now, when they have both been removed to a higher and a better sphere of existence, and when every unkind feeling has been quenched in the triumphs of the grave, this country still feels, and for years will continue to feel, the influence of those agitations to which their powerful and impressive characters gave impulse.

But I must pause. If I were to attempt to present all the aspects in which the character of this illustrious man will challenge the applause of history, I should fatigue the House and violate the just limit allowed for such remarks.

I cannot however conclude, sir, without making some more special allusion to Mr. Clay, as a native of that State which I have the honour in part to represent upon this floor. We are all proud, and very properly proud, of the distinguished men to whom our respective States have given birth. It is a just and laudable emulation, and one, in a confederated government like ours, proper to be encouraged. And while men like Mr. Clay very rapidly rise above the confined limits of a State reputation, and acquire a national fame, in which all claim and all have an equal interest, still there is a propriety and fitness in preserving the relation between the individual and his State. Virginia has given birth to a large number of men who have by their distinguished talents and services impressed their names upon the hearts and memories of their countrymen; but certainly, since the colonial era, she has given birth to no man, who, in the massive and gigantic proportions of his character, and in the splendour of his native endowments, can be compared to HENRY CLAY. At an early age he emigrated from his native State, and found a home in Kentucky. In a speech which he delivered in the Senate of the United States, in February, 1842—and which I well remember—upon the occasion of his resigning his seat in that body, he expressed the wish that, when that event should occur which has now clothed this city in mourning and filled the nation with grief, his "earthly remains should be laid under the green sod of Kentucky, with those of her gallant and patriotic sons."

Sir, however gratifying it might be to us that his remains should be transferred to his native soil, to there mingle with the ashes of Washington, Jefferson, Madison, Lee, and Henry, we cannot complain of the very natural preference which he has himself expressed. If Virginia did give him birth—Kentucky has nourished him in his manhood—has freely lavished upon him her highest honours—has shielded him from harm when the clouds of calumny and detraction gathered heavily and loweringly about him, and she has watched over his fame with the tenderness and zeal of a mother. Sir, it is not to be wondered that he should have expressed the wish he did, to be laid by the side of her gallant and patriotic sons. Happy Kentucky! Happy in having an adopted son so worthy of her highest honours. Happy, in the unshaken fidelity and loyalty with which, for near half a century, those honours have been so steadfastly and gracefully accorded to him.

Sir, whilst Virginia, in the exercise of her own proper judgment, has differed from Mr. CLAY in some of his views of national policy, she has never, at any period of his public career, failed to regard him with pride, as one of her most distinguished sons; to honour the purity and the manliness of his character, and to award to him the high credit of an honest and sincere devotion to his country's welfare. And now, sir, that death has arrested for ever the pulsations of that mighty heart, and sealed in eternal silence those eloquent lips upon whose accents thousands have so often hung in rapture, I shall stand justified in saying, that a wail of lamentation will be heard from her people—her whole people—reverberating through her mountains and valleys, as deep, as genuine, and as sincere as that, which I know, will swell the noble hearts and the heaving bosoms of the people of his own cherished, and beloved Kentucky.

Sir, as I walked to the Capitol this morning, every object which attracted my eye, admonished me that a nation's benefactor had departed from amongst us. He is gone! HENRY CLAY, the idol of his friends, the ornament of the Senate Chamber, the pride of his country; he whose presence gathered crowds of his admiring fellow-men around him, as if he had been one descended from above, has passed for ever from our view.

> "His soul, enlarged from its vile bonds, has gone
> To that REFULGENT world, where it shall swim
> In liquid light, and float on seas of bliss."

But the memory of his virtues and of his services will be gratefully embalmed in the hearts of his countrymen, and generations yet unborn will be taught to lisp with reverence and enthusiasm the name of HENRY CLAY.

Mr. PARKER, of Indiana, said:—

Mr. SPEAKER: This is a solemn—a consecrated hour. And I would not detain the members of the House from indulging in the silence of their own feelings, so grateful to hearts chastened as ours.

But I cannot restrain an expression from a bosom pained with its fulness.

When my young thoughts first took cognisance of the fact that I have a country—my eye was attracted by the magnificent proportions of HENRY CLAY.

The idea absorbed me then, that he was, above all other men, the embodiment of my country's genius.

I have watched him; I have studied him; I have admired him—and, God forgive me! for he was but a man, "of like passions with us"—I fear I have *idolized* him, until this hour.

But he has gone from among men; and it is for US now to awake and apply ourselves, with renewed fervour and increased fidelity, to the welfare of the country HE loved so well and served so truly and so long—the glorious country yet saved to us!

Yes, HENRY CLAY has fallen, at last!—as the ripe oak falls, in the stillness of the forest. But the verdant and gorgeous richness of his glories will only fade and wither from the earth, when his country's history shall have been forgotten.

"One generation passeth away and another generation cometh." Thus it has been from the beginning, and thus it will be, until time shall be no longer.

Yesterday morning, at eleven o'clock, the spirit of HENRY CLAY—so long the pride and glory of his own country, and the admiration of all the world—was yet with us, though struggling to be free. Ere "high noon" came, it had passed over "the dark river," through the gate, into the celestial city, inhabited by all the "just men made perfect."

May not our rapt vision contemplate him there, this day, in sweet communion with the dear friends that have gone before him?—with Madison, and Jefferson, and Washington, and Henry, and Franklin—with the eloquent Tully, with the "divine Plato," with Aaron the Levite, who could "speak well"—

with all the great and good, since and before the flood!

His princely tread has graced these aisles for the last time. These halls will wake no more to the magic music of his voice.

Did that tall spirit, in its etherial form, enter the courts of the upper sanctuary, bearing itself comparably with the spirits there, as was his walk among men?

Did the mellifluous tones of his greeting there enrapture the hosts of Heaven, comparably with his strains "to stir men's blood" on earth?

Then, may we not fancy, when it was announced to the inhabitants of that better country, HE COMES! —HE COMES!—there was a rustling of angel-wings—a thrilling joy—*up there*, only to be witnessed once in an earthly age?

Adieu!—a last adieu to thee, HENRY CLAY!

The hearts of all thy countrymen are melted, on this day, because of the thought that thou art gone.

Could we have held the hand of the "insatiate archer," thou hadst not died; but thou wouldst have tarried with us, in the full grandeur of thy greatness, until we had no longer need of a country.

But we thank our Heavenly Father that thou wast given to us; and that thou didst survive so long.

We would cherish thy memory while we live, as our country's JEWEL—than which none is richer.

And we will teach our children the lessons of matchless patriotism thou hast taught us; with the fond hope that our LIBERTY and our UNION may only expire with "the last of earth."

Mr. GENTRY, said:—

Mr. SPEAKER: I do not rise to pronounce an eulogy on the life and character and public services of the illustrious orator and statesman whose death this nation deplores. Suitably to perform that task, a higher eloquence than I possess might essay in vain. The gushing tears of the nation, the deep grief which oppresses the hearts of more than twenty millions of people, constitute a more eloquent eulogium upon the life and character and patriot services of HENRY CLAY, than the power of language can express. In no part of our country is that character more admired, or those public services more appreciated, than in the State which I have the honour, in part, to represent. I claim for the people of that State a full participation in the general woe which the sad announcement of to-day will everywhere inspire.

Mr. BOWIE, said:—

Mr. SPEAKER: I rise not to utter the measured phrases of premeditated woe, but to speak as my constituency would, if they stood around the grave now opening to receive the mortal remains, not of a statesman only, but of a beloved friend.

If there is a State in this Union, other than Kentucky, which sends up a wail of more bitter and sincere sorrow than another, that State is Maryland.

In her midst, the departed statesman was a frequent and a welcome guest. At many a board, and many a fireside, his noble form was the light of the eyes, the idol of the heart. Throughout her borders, in cottage, hamlet, and city, his name is a household word, his thoughts are familiar sentences.

Though not permitted to be the first at his cradle, Maryland would be the last at his tomb.

Through all the phases of political fortune, amid all the storms which darkened his career, Maryland cherished him in her inmost heart, as the most gifted, patriotic, and eloquent of men. To this hour, prayers ascend from many domestic altars, evening and morning, for his temporal comfort and eternal welfare. In the language of inspiration, Maryland would exclaim, "There is a prince and a great man, fallen this day, in Israel." Daughters of America! weep for him "who hath clothed you in scarlet and fine linen."

The husbandman at his plough, the artisan at the anvil, and the seaman on the mast, will pause and drop a tear when he hears CLAY is no more.

The advocate of Freedom in both hemispheres, he will be lamented alike on the shores of the Hellespont and the banks of the Mississippi and Orinoco. The freed men of Liberia, learning and practising the art of self-government, and civilizing Africa, have lost in him a patron and protector, a father and a friend. America mourns the eclipse of a luminary, which enlightened and illuminated the continent; the United States, a counsellor of deepest wisdom and purest purpose; mankind, the advocate of human rights and constitutional liberty.

Mr. WALSH, said:—

Mr. SPEAKER: The illustrious man whose death we this day mourn, was so long my political leader —so long almost the object of my personal idolatry —that I cannot allow that he shall go down to the grave, without a word at least of affectionate remembrance—without a tribute to a memory which will exact tribute as long as a heart shall be found to beat within the bosom of civilized man, and human agency shall be adequate in any *form* to give them an expression; and even, sir, if I had no heartfelt sigh to pour out here—if I had no tear for that coffin's lid, I should do injustice to those whose representative in part I am, if I did not in this *presence*, and at this time, raise the voice to swell the accents of the profoundest public sorrow.

The State of Maryland has always vied with Kentucky in love and adoration of his name. Her people have gathered around him with all the fervour of a first affection, and with more than its *duration*. Troops of friends have ever clustered about his pathway with a personal devotion which each man of them regarded as the highest individual honour—friends, sir, to whose firesides the tidings of his death will go with all the withering influences which are felt when household ties are severed.

I wish, sir, I could offer now a proper memorial for such a subject and such an affection. But as I strive to utter it, I feel the disheartening influence of the well-known truth, that in view of death all minds sink into triteness. It would seem, indeed, sir, that the great leveller of our race would vindicate his *title* to be so considered, by making all men think alike in regard to his visitation—"the thousand thoughts that begin and end in one"—the *desolation* here—the eternal hope *hereafter*—are influences felt alike by the lowest intellect and the loftiest genius.

Mr. Speaker, a statesman for more than fifty years in the councils of his country, whose peculiar charge it was to see that the Republic suffered no detriment—a patriot for all times, all circumstances, and all emergencies—has passed away from the trials and triumphs of the world, and gone to his reward. Sad as are the emotions which such an event would ordinarily excite, their intensity is heightened by the matters so fresh within the memories of us all:

> "Oh! think how to his latest day,
> When death, just hovering, claim'd his prey,
> With Palinurus' unalter'd mood,
> Firm at his dangerous post he stood,

Each call for needful rest repell'd,
With dying hand the rudder held;
Then while on freedom's thousand plains
One unpolluted church remains,
Whose peaceful bells ne'er sent around
The bloody tocsin's maddening sound,
But still, upon the hallow'd day,
Convoke the swains to praise and pray,
While faith and civil peace are dear,
Greet his cold marble with a tear,
He who preserved them—CLAY lies here."

In a character, Mr. Speaker, so illustrious and beautiful, it is difficult to select any point for particular notice, from those which go to make up its noble proportions; but we may now, around his honoured grave, call to grateful recollection that invincible spirit which no personal sorrow could sully, and no disaster could overcome. Be assured, sir, that he has in this regard left a legacy to the young men of the Republic, almost as sacred and as dear as that liberty of which his life was a blessed illustration.

We can all remember, sir, when adverse political results disheartened his friends, and made them feel even as men without hope, that his own clarion voice was still heard in the purpose and the pursuit of right, as bold and as eloquent as when it first proclaimed the freedom of the seas, and its talismanic tones struck off the badges of bondage from the lands of the Incas, and the plains of Marathon.

Mr. Speaker, in the exultation of the statesman he did not forget the duties of the man. He was an affectionate adviser on all points wherein inexperienced youth might require counsel. He was a disinterested sympathizer in personal sorrows that called for consolation. He was ever upright and honourable in all the duties incident to his relations in life.

To an existence so lovely, Heaven in its mercy granted a fitting and appropriate close. It was the prayer, Mr. Speaker, of a distinguished citizen, who died some years since in the metropolis, even while his spirit was fluttering for its final flight, that he might depart gracefully. It may not be presumptuous to say, that what was in that instance the aspiration of a chivalric *gentleman*, was in this the realization of the dying *Christian*, in which was blended all that human dignity could require, with all that Divine grace had conferred; in which the firmness of the man was only transcended by the fervour of the penitent.

A short period before his death he remarked to one by his bedside, "that he was fearful he was becoming selfish, as his thoughts were entirely withdrawn from the world and centred upon eternity." This, sir, was but the purification of his noble spirit from all the dross of earth—a happy illustration of what the religious muse has so sweetly sung—

"No sin to stain—no lure to stay
The soul, as home she springs;
Thy sunshine on her joyful way,
Thy freedom in her wings."

Mr. Speaker, the solemnities of this hour may soon be forgotten. We may come back from the new-made grave only still to show that we consider "eternity the bubble, life and time the enduring substance." We may not pause long enough by the brink to ask which of us revellers of to-day shall next be at rest. But be assured, sir, that upon the records of mortality will never be inscribed a name more illustrious than that of the statesman, patriot, and friend whom the nation mourns.

The question was then put on the adoption of the resolutions proposed by Mr. BRECKINRIDGE, and they were unanimously adopted.

ORDER OF PROCEEDINGS AT THE FUNERAL

OF THE

HON. HENRY CLAY,

A SENATOR OF THE UNITED STATES FROM THE STATE OF KENTUCKY.

THURSDAY, JULY 1, 1852.

THE Committee of Arrangements, Pall-Bearers and Mourners, attended at the National Hotel, the late residence of the deceased, at 11 o'clock, A. M. At half-past eleven the funeral procession to the Capitol was formed, in the following order:—

The Chaplains of both Houses of Congress.

Physicians who attended the deceased.

Committee of Arrangements.

Mr. HUNTER,	Mr. COOPER,
Mr. DAWSON,	Mr. BRIGHT,
Mr. JONES, of Iowa,	Mr. SMITH.

Pall-Bearers.

Mr. CASS,	CORPSE.	Mr. PRATT,
Mr. MANGUM,		Mr. ATCHISON,
Mr. DODGE, of Wis.		Mr. BELL.

Committee to attend the remains of the deceased to Kentucky:—

Mr. UNDERWOOD,	Mr. FISH,
Mr. JONES, of Tenn.	Mr. HOUSTON,
Mr. CASS,	Mr. STOCKTON.

The Family and Friends of the deceased.

The Senators and Representatives from the State of Kentucky, as mourners.

The Sergeant-at-Arms of the Senate.

The Senate of the United States, preceded by their President *pro tempore*, and Secretary.

The other Officers of the Senate.

The Sergeant-at-Arms of the House of Representatives.

The House of Representatives, preceded by their Speaker and Clerk.

The other Officers of the House of Representatives.

Judges of the United States.

Officers of the Executive Departments.

Officers of the Army and Navy.

The Mayor and Corporation of Washington, and of other Cities.

Civic Associations.

Military Companies.

Citizens and Strangers.

The procession having entered the Senate Chamber, where the President of the United States, the Heads of Departments, the Diplomatic Corps, and others were already present, the funeral service was performed by Rev. Dr. Butler, Chaplain to the Senate.

At the conclusion of the service, the corpse was placed in the Rotunda, where it remained until half-past three o'clock, P. M., when it was removed, in charge of the Committee of Arrangements and Pall-Bearers, to the Railroad Depot, and confided to the Committee appointed to accompany it to Kentucky.

The Strong Staff broken and the Beautiful Rod.

A SERMON

DELIVERED IN THE SENATE CHAMBER OF THE UNITED STATES,
JULY 1, 1852,

ON THE OCCASION OF THE

FUNERAL OF THE HON. HENRY CLAY,

BY THE

REV. C. M. BUTLER, D.D.
CHAPLAIN OF THE SENATE.

SERMON.

"How is the strong staff broken, and the beautiful rod!"—Jer. xlviii. 17.

Before all hearts and minds in this august assemblage the vivid image of *one man* stands. To some aged eye he may come forth, from the dim past, as he appeared in the neighbouring city of his native State, a lithe and ardent youth, full of promise, of ambition, and of hope. To another he may appear as, in a distant State, in the courts of justice, erect, high-strung, bold, wearing the fresh forensic laurel on his young and open brow. Some may see him in the earlier, and some in the later, stages of his career, on this conspicuous theatre of his renown; and to the former he will start out on the background of the past, as he appeared in the neighbouring chamber, tall, elate, impassioned—with flashing eye, and suasive gesture, and clarion voice, an already acknowledged "Agamemnon, King of Men;" and to others he will again stand in this chamber, "the strong staff" of the bewildered and staggering State, and "the beautiful rod," rich with the blossoms of genius, and of patriotic love and hope, the life of youth still remaining to give animation, grace, and exhaustless vigour, to the wisdom, the experience, and the gravity of age. To others he may be present as he sat in the chamber of sickness, cheerful, majestic, gentle—his mind clear, his heart warm, his hope fixed on Heaven, peacefully preparing for his last great change. To the memory of the minister of God he appears as the penitent, humble, and peaceful Christian, who received him with the affection of a father, and joined with him in solemn sacrament and prayer, with the gentleness of a woman, and the humility of a child. "Out of the strong came forth sweetness." "How is the strong staff broken, and the beautiful rod!"

But not before this Assembly only, does the venerated image of the departed Statesman, this day, distinctly stand. For more than a thousand miles—east, west, north, and south—it is known and remembered, that at this place and hour, a nation's Representatives assemble to do honour to him whose fame is now a nation's heritage. A nation's mighty heart throbs against this Capitol, and beats through you. In many cities banners droop, bells toll, cannons boom, funereal draperies wave. In crowded streets and on sounding wharfs, upon steamboats and upon cars, in fields and in workshops, in homes, in schools, millions of men, women, and children have their thoughts fixed upon this scene, and say mournfully to each other, "This is the hour in which, at the Capitol, the nation's Representatives are burying HENRY CLAY." *Burying* HENRY CLAY! Bury the records of your country's history—bury the hearts of living millions—bury the mountains, the rivers, the lakes, and the spreading lands from sea to sea, with which his name is inseparably associated, and even then you would not bury HENRY CLAY—for he lives in other lands, and speaks in other tongues, and to other times than our's.

A great mind, a great heart, a great orator, a great career, have been consigned to history. She will record his rare gifts of deep insight, keen discrimination, clear statement, rapid combination, plain, direct, and convincing logic. She will love to dwell on that large, generous, magnanimous, open, forgiving heart. She will linger, with fond delight, on the recorded and traditional stories of an eloquence that was so masterful and stirring, because it was but *himself*, struggling to come forth on the living words —because, though the words were brave and strong, and beautiful and melodious, it was felt that, behind them there was a *soul* braver, stronger, more beautiful, and more melodious, than language could express. She will point to a career of statesmanship which has, to a remarkable degree, stamped itself on the public policy of the country, and reached, in beneficent practical results, the fields, the looms, the commercial marts, and the quiet homes of all the land, where his name was, with the departed fathers, and is with the living children, and will be, with successive generations, an honoured household word.

I feel, as a man, the grandeur of this career. But as an immortal, with this broken wreck of mortality, before me, with this scene as the "end-all" of human glory, I feel that no career is truly great but that of him who, whether he be illustrious or obscure, lives to the future in the present, and linking himself to the spiritual world, draws from God the life, the rule, the motive, and the reward of all his labour. So would that great spirit which has departed say to us, could he address us now. So did he realize, in the calm and meditative close of life. I feel that I but utter the lessons which, living, were his last and best convictions, and which, dead, would be, could he speak to us, his solemn admonitions, when I say that statesmanship is then only glorious, when it is *Christian:* and that man is then only safe, and true to his duty, and his soul, when the life which he lives in the flesh is the life of faith in the Son of God.

Great, indeed, is the privilege, and most honourable and useful is the career, of a Christian American statesman. He perceives that civil liberty came from the freedom wherewith Christ made its early martyrs and defenders free. He recognises it as one of the twelve manner of fruits on the Tree of Life, which, while its lower branches furnish the best nutriment of earth, hangs on its topmost boughs, which wave in Heaven, fruits that exhilarate the immortals. Recognising the State as God's institution, he will perceive that his own ministry is divine. Living consciously under the eye, and in the love and fear of God; redeemed by the blood of Jesus; sanctified by His Spirit; loving His law; he will give himself, in private and in public, to the service of his Saviour. He will not admit that he may act on less lofty principles in public, than in private life; and that he must be careful of his moral influence in the small sphere of home and neighbourhood, but need take no heed of it when it stretches over continents and crosses seas. He will know that his moral responsibility cannot be divided and distributed among others. When he is told that adherence to the strictest moral and religious principle is incompatible with a successful and eminent career, he will denounce the assertion as a libel on the venerated Fathers of the Republic—a libel on the honoured living and the illustrious dead—a libel against a great and Christian nation—a libel against God himself, who has declared and made "godliness profitable for the life that now is." He will strive to make laws the transcripts of the character, and institutions illustrations of the providence of God. He will scan with admiration and awe the purposes of God in the future history of the world, in throwing open this wide

Continent, from sea to sea, as the abode of freedom, intelligence, plenty, prosperity, and peace; and feel that in giving his energies with a patriot's love, to the welfare of his country, he is consecrating himself, with a Christian's zeal, to the extension and establishment of the Redeemer's kingdom. Compared with a career like this, which is equally open to those whose public sphere is large or small, how paltry are the trade of patriotism, the tricks of statesmanship, the rewards of successful baseness! This hour, this scene, the venerated dead, the country, the world, the present, the future, God, duty, Heaven, hell, speak trumpet-tongued to all in the service of their country, to *beware* how they lay polluted or unhallowed hands

> "Upon the ark
> Of her magnificent and awful cause!"

Such is the character of that statesmanship which alone would have met the full approval of the venerated dead. For the religion which always had a place in the convictions of his mind, had also, within a recent period, entered into his experience, and seated itself in his heart. Twenty years since he wrote—"I am a member of no religious sect, and I am not a professor of religion. I regret that I am not. I wish that I was, and trust that I shall be. I have, and always have had, a profound regard for

Christianity, the religion of my fathers, and for its rites, its usages, and observances." That feeling proved that the seed sown by pious parents, was not dead though stifled. A few years since, its dormant life was re-awakened. He was baptized in the communion of the Protestant Episcopal Church; and during his sojourn in this city, he was in full communion with Trinity Parish.

It is since his withdrawal from the sittings of the Senate, that I have been made particularly acquainted with his religious opinions, character, and feelings. From the commencement of his illness he always expressed to me his persuasion that its termination would be fatal. From that period until his death, it was my privilege to hold frequent religious services and conversations with him in his room. He avowed to me his full faith in the great leading doctrines of the Gospel—the fall and sinfulness of man, the divinity of Christ, the reality and necessity of the Atonement, the need of being born again by the Spirit, and salvation through faith in a crucified Redeemer. His own personal hopes of salvation, he ever and distinctly based on the promises and the grace of Christ. Strikingly perceptible, on his naturally impetuous and impatient character, was the influence of grace in producing submission, and "a patient waiting for Christ," and for death. On one occasion he spoke to me of the pious example of one very near and dear to him, as that which led him deeply to feel, and earnestly to seek for himself, the reality and the blessedness of religion. On another occasion, he told me that he had been striving to form a conception of Heaven; and he enlarged upon the mercy of that provision by which our Saviour became a partaker of our humanity, that our hearts and hopes might fix themselves on him. On another occasion, when he was supposed to be very near his end, I expressed to him the hope that his mind and heart were at peace, and that he was able to rest with cheerful confidence on the promises, and in the merits of the Redeemer. He said, with much feeling, that he endeavoured to, and trusted that he did repose his salvation upon Christ; that it was too late for him to look at Christianity in the light of speculation; that he had never doubted of its truth; and that he now wished to throw himself upon it as a practical and blessed remedy. Very soon after this, I administered to him the sacrament of the Lord's Supper. Being extremely feeble, and desirous of having his mind undiverted, no persons were present, but his son and his servant. It was a scene long to be remembered. There, in that still chamber, at a week-day noon, the tides of life flowing all around us, three disciples of the Saviour, the minister of God, the dying statesman, and his servant, a partaker of the like precious faith, commemorated their Saviour's dying love. He joined in the blessed sacrament with great feeling and solemnity, now pressing his hands together, and now spreading them forth, as the words of the service expressed the feelings, desires, supplications, confessions, and thanksgivings, of his heart. His eyes were dim with grateful tears, his heart was full of peace and love! After this he rallied, and again I was permitted frequently to join with him in religious services, conversation, and prayer. He grew in grace and in the knowledge of our Lord and Saviour Jesus Christ. Among the books which, in connection with the Word of God, he read most, were "Jay's Morning and Evening Exercises," the "Life of Dr. Chalmers," and "The Christian Philosopher Triumphant in Death." His hope continued to the end to be, though true and real, tremulous with humility rather than rapturous with assurance. When he felt most the weariness of his protracted sufferings, it sufficed to suggest to him that his Heavenly Father doubtless knew, that after a life so long and stirring, and tempted, such a discipline of chastening and suffering was needful to make him more meet for the inheritance of the saints—and at once words of meek and patient acquiescence escaped his lips.

Exhausted nature at length gave way. On the last occasion, when I was permitted to offer a brief prayer at his bedside, his last words to me were that he had hope only in Christ, and that the prayer which I had offered for his pardoning love, and his sanctifying grace, included every thing which the dying need. On the evening previous to his departure, sitting for an hour in silence by his side, I could not but realize, when I heard him, in the slight wanderings of his mind to other days, and other scenes, murmuring the words, "*My mother! Mother! Mother!*" and saying "*My dear wife!*" as if she were present, and frequently uttering aloud, as if in response to some silent Litany of the soul, the simple prayer, "Lord, have mercy upon me!"—I could not but realize then, and rejoice to think how near was the blessed reunion of his weary heart with the loved dead, and with her — Our dear Lord gently smooth her passage to the tomb!—who must soon follow him to his rest—whose spirits even then seemed to visit, and to cheer his memory and his hope. Gently he breathed his soul away into the spirit world.

"How blest the righteous when they die!
When holy souls retire to rest,
How mildly beams the closing eye,
How gently heaves the expiring breast!

"So fades the summer cloud away,
So sinks the gale when storms are o'er,
So gently shuts the eye of day,
So dies the wave upon the shore!"

Be it ours to follow him, in the same humble and submissive faith, to Heaven. Could he speak to us the counsels of his latest human, and his present Heavenly, experience, sure I am that he would not only admonish us to cling to the Saviour, in sickness and in death: but abjure us not to delay to act upon our first convictions, that we might give our best powers and fullest influence to God, and go to the grave with a hope, unshadowed by the long worldliness of the past, or by the films of fear and doubt resting over the future.

The strong staff is broken, and the beautiful rod is despoiled of its grace and bloom ; but in the light of the eternal promises, and by the power of Christ's resurrection, we joyfully anticipate the prospect of seeing that broken staff erect, and that beautiful rod clothed with celestial grace, and blossoming with undying life and blessedness in the Paradise of God.

THE END.

www.ingramcontent.com/pod-product-compliance
Lightning Source LLC
LaVergne TN
LVHW021415110826
845150LV00007B/1942

* 9 7 8 1 4 2 5 5 0 9 9 8 9 *